"So many of us who work with young people have been asking for a manual exactly like this one. It is full of practical examples, easy-to-understand science, and engaging exercises ideal for high school students, mental health professionals, and parents who are keen to help teens improve their resilience. Integrating new ideas about individual resilience, Bradshaw offers readers a tool for self-reflection and a deeper understanding of how stress and self-doubt make teens vulnerable. It's a great resource, ideal for both clinical and educational settings."

—**Michael Ungar, PhD**, author of *Change Your World*; Canada research chair in child, family, and community resilience; and professor of social work at Dalhousie University in Halifax, NS, Canada

"Cheryl is an amazing, relatable, and down-to-earth psychotherapist. Her book is easy to follow, funny, and captures the most up-to-date strategies in mental health. Strategies such as self-care, mindfulness, goal setting, and cognitive behavioral therapy (CBT) make this a go-to book for any adolescent—one struggling with everyday issues or one who is struggling with more persistent mental health concerns. Cheryl makes the reader feel as though she is talking to them one-on-one. The exercises make the book fun. A good self-help book for teens, or a great resource to be used in conjunction with therapy."

—**Quynn Morehouse, PsyD**, clinical psychologist in private practice in Portland, ME

"*The Resilience Workbook for Teens* is an interesting, important, and fun guide for young people to develop their resilience skills in the face of an ever-growing stressful world. Cheryl Bradshaw has created exercises that are highly engaging. I would highly recommend this book to teens and those who work with teens. Can't wait to use the workbook with my clients!"

—**Caren Baruch-Feldman, PhD**, psychologist and author of *The Grit Guide for Teens*

"In our world today, many youths lack the ability to face challenging situations without becoming overwhelmed, often resulting in escalating stress, anxiety, and depression. *The Resilience Workbook for Teens* offers a full array of different types of activities to help teens gain confidence in their ability to traverse emotionally charged situations, face their fears, be vulnerable, and come out on top. Writing exercises allow readers to articulate their own feelings and values, and checklists offer specific ways in which readers can directly take care of themselves when energy is low. A great resource for all teens!"

—**Karen Bluth, PhD**, assistant professor in the department of psychiatry, and fellow at the Frank Porter Graham Child Development Institute at the University of North Carolina, Chapel Hill; and author of *The Self-Compassion Workbook for Teens*

"Adolescence can be a challenging time for many individuals, and learning to adapt and be resilient in the face of so many changes can be especially difficult. The good news is that resilience is a set of skills that can be learned. In *The Resilience Workbook for Teens*, Cheryl Bradshaw has transformed resiliency skill building into practical, engaging, and memorable activities to help you learn to bounce back from whatever life throws your way. Her writing is clear, charming, and engaging. Cheryl's warmth and compassion shows through as though she is in the room with you, guiding you on your journey."

—**Sheri Turrell, PhD**, clinical psychologist working with teens and adults in Toronto, ON, Canada; Association for Contextual Behavioral Science (ACBS) peer-reviewed ACT trainer; and coauthor of *ACT for Adolescents*

"What an incredible resource! Cheryl's warm and down-to-earth voice provides an engaging invitation for teens (and their parents) to understand themselves more deeply. Through metaphors and powerful stories, Cheryl helps teens understand that they are not alone in feeling like their inner landscape sometimes seems like unfriendly territory. This book provides a clear road map and simple, fun activities for anyone who is ready to understand the patterns they've been in, see their own inner strength, and embrace who they are. I'm so excited to share this book with my clients!"

—**Deanne Barrett, MA**, teenage expert and life coach, founder of HeartShift Club for Moms of Teens, and director of Gratitudeworks Enterprises Inc. in Calgary, AB, Canada

"In *The Resilience Workbook for Teens*, Cheryl M. Bradshaw has achieved the impossible. She has written an evidence-based workbook on building resilience that will intrigue teens and effectively help them develop the factors that foster resilience. In a voice that is present and personal, she seems to be sitting next to the teen as she makes sense of theory, acknowledges resistance to change, and then makes change possible in small, interesting steps set up in a workbook format. Cheryl clearly knows teens and knows how to engage them in developing resilience. Her book is a contribution to teen development."

> —**Suzanne B. Phillips, PsyD, ABPP**, psychologist, psychoanalyst, coauthor
> of *Healing Together*, and host of *Psych Up Live* on International Talk Radio

"Achieving success in any arena stems from having grit, and *The Resilience Workbook for Teens* is a wonderful resource. Cheryl Bradshaw knows how young people think and work, and she has written an engaging and practical how-to book that contains a wealth of strategies and activities that will develop self-awareness and lead to resilience. These pages facilitate reflection, analysis, and action. I am sure that it will be very helpful to any young person (and be useful to not-so-young people, too!)."

> —**Thomas R. Hoerr, PhD**, emeritus head of the New City School; scholar
> in residence at the University of Missouri–St. Louis; and author of
> *The Formative Five*

"Engaging and transformative! *The Resilience Workbook for Teens* fuses acceptance and commitment therapy (ACT), dialectical behavior therapy (DBT), and CBT in the perfect recipe for change. An essential resource that delivers the ingredients and fosters hunger for teens to make meaningful change in the relationship they have with themselves!"

> —**Erin Lipsitt, MSW, RSW**, counselor/therapist at the University of Guelph,
> and mother of teens

"In *The Resilience Workbook for Teens*, Cheryl brilliantly pulls together a range of activities and tools that have helped me better understand myself; it is a book every young person needs to read. As a young adult trying to figure out my purpose and where I fit in this world, this accessible, practical, and easy-to-read guide allowed me to work these things through, alongside an author who felt like not only a mental health professional, but a confidant and friend who wanted absolutely nothing but the best for me. Anyone, at any age, can learn something from the concepts, ideas, and activities in this book. I wish I could hand this to my younger self, and would encourage anyone reading this to share it with all the young people in your life."

> —**Jessica Fazio**, youth mental health advocate and speaker, www.jack.org network representative alumna, IAYMH executive member, and passionate leader and changemaker

"This workbook couldn't come at a better time! Another valuable and needed resource for practitioners and parents from author and psychotherapist Cheryl Bradshaw. With an overwhelming number of teens suffering from anxiety and low self-esteem today, it's essential we provide them with tools, in addition to our support, to help them cultivate resilience. This book provides just that: practical and educational support to help our teens develop the skills needed to thrive in the face of adversity and challenges. Cheryl knows her stuff!"

> —**Laura Dobrinsky, BSc, DC**, family health and wellness expert; and Brain Care is Self-Care™ mentor/speaker

"In *The Resilience Workbook for Teens*, Cheryl Bradshaw offers an insightful, compassionate, and practical plan for regaining and maintaining mental wellness. The goals are achievable, the activities are engaging, and the explanations are straightforward and accessible. This is a valuable read for young people, as well as for those who work with and care about them."

> —**Mark Henick**, mental health strategist, and Top 50 TEDx Speaker

the resilience workbook for teens

activities to help you gain
confidence, manage stress &
cultivate a growth mindset

CHERYL M. BRADSHAW, MA

Instant Help Books
An Imprint of New Harbinger Publications, Inc.

Publisher's Note

Distributed in Canada by Raincoast Books

Copyright © 2019 by Cheryl M. Bradshaw
        Instant Help Books
        An imprint of New Harbinger Publications, Inc.
        5674 Shattuck Avenue
        Oakland, CA 94609
        www.newharbinger.com

Cover design by Amy Shoup

Acquired by Elizabeth Hollis Hansen

Edited by Ken Knabb

Library of Congress Cataloging-in-Publication Data

Names: Bradshaw, Cheryl M., author.
Title: The resilience workbook for teens : activities to help you gain confidence, manage stress, and
    cultivate a growth mindset / Cheryl Bradshaw.
Description: Oakland, CA : New Harbinger Publications, Inc., [2019] | Includes bibliographical references.
Identifiers: LCCN 2019022148 (print) | LCCN 2019980886 (ebook) | ISBN 9781684032921 (paperback) |
    ISBN 9781684032938 (pdf) | ISBN 9781684032945 (epub)
Subjects: LCSH: Resilience (Personality trait) in adolescence--Juvenile literature. | Stress management--
    Juvenile literature.
Classification: LCC BF724.3.R47 B73 2019 (print) | LCC BF724.3.R47 (ebook) | DDC 155.5/1824--dc23
LC record available at https://lccn.loc.gov/2019022148
LC ebook record available at https://lccn.loc.gov/2019980886

Printed in the United States of America

23   22   21

10   9   8   7   6   5   4   3

To every student and client I have worked with in counselling:

You have each taught me something different about strength and resilience through your willingness to show up, do the work, and talk about life's greatest struggles. I thank each of you for the opportunity to have worked with you.

contents

a note for educators, mental health professionals, and parents

Thanks for picking up this book! The goals and exercises in this book are aimed to build different personal traits that have been shown to contribute to emotional and psychological resilience.

"Resilience" means being able to withstand difficult times, challenging times, and adversity. But how does one measure that? As we try to narrow in on a workable definition, Peres, Moreira-Almeida, Nasello, and Koenig (2007) give us a good starting point, defining resilience as the ability to go through challenges and difficulties and to then still regain a satisfactory quality of life. They have linked this concept to creating a new sense of meaning and purpose in one's life as a result of going through challenging experiences without remaining fixated on the negative aspects of those experiences.

Other qualities that are discussed frequently in the literature are self-efficacy (Margolis & McCabe, 2006), high self-esteem, internal locus of control, external attributions of blame, optimism, determination in the face of obstacles, cognitive flexibility and reappraisal ability, social competence, and the ability to face fears (Cicchetti & Rogosch, 2009).

While we're seeking to help people build resilience with all these different impacts and factors, we want to know that the tools we are giving people are actually accomplishing this goal. For this purpose, we look at the scales that researchers use to measure levels of resilience. There are more than nineteen different psychometric tools to quantitatively track and measure the trait of resilience in youth and adults. A study conducted by Windle, Bennett, and Noyes (2011) reviewed fifteen of these, and found that the top choice was the Connor-Davidson Resilience Scale (Connor & Davidson, 2003).

The Connor-Davidson Resilience Scale (CD-RISC) is a twenty-five-item scale that measures the ability to "thrive in the face of adversity." However, it has been found that a ten-item CD-RISC, which took the twenty-five-item scale and condensed it for accuracy, reliability, and validity, is likely the most accurate measure of resilience to date (Aloba, Olabisi, & Aloba, 2016; Campbell-Sills & Stein, 2007). The ten items on that scale consider the following general themes: self-efficacy, sense of humor, secure attachment to others, the ability to adapt to change, commitment, control, thinking of change as a challenge, patience, the ability to tolerate stress and pain, and optimism and faith

(Connor & Davidson, 2003). These themes have been a guide to the activities included in this workbook—to ensure that the skills we will work on here will target the areas that research tells us best increase resilience.

Resilience theorists suggest that many of the skills listed above are neurologically modifiable to a measureable level through therapeutic approaches such as cognitive behavioral therapy (CBT), acceptance and commitment therapy (ACT), and dialectical behavior therapy (DBT) (Kalisch, Müller, & Tüscher, 2015). Recent research has been able to show at the neurological level that teaching people to think of issues in different ways—to reframe them in positive terms when the initial response is negative, or in a less emotional way when the initial response is highly emotional—changes how people experience and react to those same issues after the skill is taught. This shows that therapy can and does work—people can learn to better regulate their emotions, and the skill development seems to have lasting effects (Doré, Weber, & Ochsner, 2017).

In fact, the therapy approaches of CBT, ACT, DBT, EMDR, narrative therapy, existential therapy, logotherapy, and mindfulness-based therapy have all been developed through rigorous study and are evidence-based approaches that help build these types of skills and traits. Activities and philosophies from each of these approaches are used in the various exercises throughout this book to help the reader in these various resilience measurement areas, giving them a good foundation to building their resilience to tackle anything that life may throw at them (Cicchetti & Rogosch, 2009; Peres, Moreira-Almeida, Nasello, & Koenig, 2007; Margolis & McCabe, 2006).

While this book addresses these internal skills, there are, of course, other areas at a broader external level that this book cannot hope to cover. These include broader community factors that have been shown to play a large role in influencing a person's resilience, including the presence and availability of a caring professional, family member, or friend to listen and help foster self-efficacy and reduction of stress (Traub & Boynton-Jarrett, 2017; Siqueira & Diaz, 2004). This is where you as the parent, teacher, or mentor come in! You can not only help in supporting the reader of this book in working on these skills through these exercises, but you can also help through your relationship with that person. A caring, nonjudgmental, empathetic, and supportive mentor in a young person's life can be instrumental in helping that person develop these tools. So keep being awesome—supporting and helping your young person through their journey!

Hi! I'm Cheryl Bradshaw, Registered Psychotherapist. I'm excited to work through this book with you! Sometimes it helps to know a bit about the author you are working through these exercises with, so let me tell you a bit about myself. I have worked with students as a counselor in college and university settings for about seven years, as well as with teens and their parents in my private practice in Waterdown, Ontario. But I didn't always start out in counseling. Let me tell you a bit about how I came to be doing this kind of work today.

I started my career in teaching. I wanted to make a difference in young people's lives, and I thought that teaching was the best way that I could influence the lives of young people on a daily basis. I created interesting and engaging lesson plans, labs, and experiments—the works. At the same time, I always tried to incorporate lessons on bullying, body image, the media, and mental wellness.

Then one day while teaching a tenth-grade frog-dissection lab, one of my female students collapsed to the ground. She began to have a seizure, with her eyes rolling back and foaming at the mouth. We evacuated the other students and immediately called for medical help and paramedics.

I stayed with the student until the paramedics arrived. As they took over, she started to come back around to consciousness. As they worked to stabilize her, they asked her questions, trying to figure out what had happened to her. After several questions, she disclosed that she had tried to end her life earlier that day in the girl's washroom, and that she had experienced physical aftereffects of this attempt while in our classroom later that day.

She was taken into medical care from our classroom and she recovered from this experience. The other teacher and I were then left to debrief with the rest of the class the next day. The student who had tried to take her life had contacted us, and had a message that she wanted us to share with the class. This is what she said: "I want to tell you that I am okay. I want you to know that now that I have gone through this—suicide is not the answer. I want anyone who is feeling this way to reach out and get help, today." As we read this message out loud to the class, I could see several students' heads drop, and their shoulders slump—I could tell that this message had hit them hard. I could almost feel the emotions that some of them felt, and it seemed obvious from this reaction I was seeing in them that they had likely felt very low themselves, either recently or at some other time in their lives, or had possibly even thought of suicide themselves at some point, too.

I started to think—how could I stand up in front of a class and teach about the circulatory system, when some of my students weren't even sure that they wanted to live to see the next day? I started to rethink the best way that I could have an impact on young people's lives, and people's lives in general. I wanted to help. I wanted to talk with them about these real and serious issues in their lives. For me, teaching was no longer the best way I felt able to do this, so I changed course and pursued a career in counseling, with a goal to work with young people and with a hope to reach as many people as I could—young and old together—through this work. For me, the more I looked, and the deeper I looked, the more I saw that mental health, emotional awareness, and emotional skills and intelligence really underpin every single thing that we do. Our ability to learn, to relate, and at times even to function, rests on our mental health and well-being, and especially on many of the skills that are related to resilience in this book.

My previous book, *How to Like Yourself* (2016), has come out of this journey as well—out of working with so many young people who are struggling with self-esteem, emotions, and mood. This *Resilience Workbook* complements *How to Like Yourself* by building and expanding on some of those ideas and concepts and providing exercises to practice some of those skills, but it is also a great stand-alone tool to build skills, learn concepts, and practice strategies that help develop resilience. I hope you enjoy doing the activities in this book as much as I enjoyed writing it!

resilience — what is it?

Resilience is a term used in many ways by many people. Some people have talked about it in the past as a trait that you are born with and that you can't change, but the good news is, most recent research suggests that it is actually something you *can* learn as a skill. And let me tell you—it's a super important skill.

Resilience has been described as "the capacity to bounce back, to withstand hardship, and to repair yourself" (Wolin & Wolin, 1993) through difficult times in life.

No matter who you are, and no matter how lucky you are in life, tough things are going to happen. People are going to get sick, friends are going to move away, breakups are going to happen, people are not going to like you, and disappointments will happen.

Even if you do "everything right," this stuff happens to everyone. And it is *hard*—no matter who you are. It's hard for adults, for parents, for teachers, for people old and young. But there are things you can learn and do, things that can build skills and a mindset and a relationship with yourself to help you get through anything—even the hardest things that life can throw at you.

Whether you are reading this book because you are starting a new school, or moving away, or your parents are separating, or you are having trouble with friends or with a romantic relationship, or anything else tough that is showing up in your life right now, I'm glad you're here with me to learn and try new things. All these exercises are ones that I have done with people anywhere from ages 12 to 70 years old—you are never too old to learn this stuff! So hopefully you are getting a head start, and can carry these skills, ideas, and exercises with you through all the next stages of your life. And I hope that you have a little bit of fun while you do it too!

Each activity has three sections—a "Let's Get Started" section, a "Let's Try It" section, and a "More to Try" section with additional skills and activities. The "Let's Get Started" section frames the idea or concept we will be working with, and gives you an idea of why it's important or how we're going to try to work with an idea to build on it or practice it. The "Let's Try It" section is where you get to grab that pen or pencil and make some of your own notes, answer questions, or maybe even draw a few things (as best you can!). The "More to Try" section might leave you with a few extra thoughts, a few extra questions, or one last activity to try. Feel free to add thoughts in the margins, make notes on additional questions, or jot down anything that feels right—venting, processing, lists, pictures…anything! It doesn't have to be perfect, and it's not going to be graded, so make mistakes, be messy, do whatever feels right. And if there's something you get stuck on, I encourage you to take this book to your parents, a mentor, or a guidance counselor or therapist (if you are seeing one) for a helping hand.

before we start

Let's get a sense of where you are starting from in the wide world of resilience, so that when we round out and complete this book together, you can look back at this moment and see how things have changed. This is a no-judgment moment! It's just going to be a short quiz we can come back to later. This is an informal quiz, modified for our purposes here from Schiraldi (2017), to get a feel for some of the pieces that are important for resilience that we are going to work on together. For each of the items listed on the left, I want you to circle the number that you feel best fits how you feel about each item, from 0 (completely false) to 4 (completely true).

Statement	Rating
I generally feel strong and capable of overcoming challenges.	0...1...2....3...4
When I get stressed, I usually bounce back fairly quickly.	0...1...2....3...4
I generally stay calm and steady when the going gets tough.	0...1...2....3...4
I am generally flexible, meaning if my usual way of doing things isn't working, I am ready and willing to try something else.	0...1...2....3...4
I am able to see that even the most difficult situations will pass, using humor or optimism to see the "big picture" of my life.	0...1...2....3...4
I like myself for who I am inside and think well of myself.	0...1...2....3...4
Difficult times don't change the way I feel about myself for the worse.	0...1...2....3...4
I know when to seek help or support, and where to find it.	0...1...2....3...4
I am good at reaching out and connecting with people when I need support.	0...1...2....3...4
I usually try to solve my problems, but I know how to accept and cope if something is beyond my control, even when it's hard.	0...1...2....3...4
I anticipate difficult situations, make a plan, and stay focused and carry out my plan even when stressed.	0...1...2....3...4
I am good at coping with strong negative emotions.	0...1...2....3...4
I have goals and am optimistic about my future, even if I run into obstacles.	0...1...2....3...4
I believe I've grown stronger from what I've experienced, and that stress can make me a stronger person.	0...1...2....3...4
I don't beat myself up when my best efforts don't succeed.	0...1...2....3...4
I stay focused and think clearly under pressure. I am persistent, determined, and resolved.	0...1...2....3...4
Total Score (add the scores from the right-hand column):	

Great! Now don't worry—whether you circled all 4's, all 0's, or somewhere in between—the goal of working through this book isn't about where you start from. It's going to be how you feel about yourself and your abilities to get through the tough things in life that matter after we're done. We will revisit these questions again after we have worked through the exercises in this book. So let's get started!

Goal 1

Adapting to Change

1 rewiring the brain

let's get started

The first thing to know about your brain is that it is awesome! I'm not kidding. That thing is a brilliant masterpiece...even if it sometimes feels like it is working against you. When you start to look at what the brain does and why, even the frustrating bits of your brain are actually pretty amazing.

One of the first things our brain does is try to make every single thing we do more efficient. Your brain is like a computer, where, like in Windows (sorry, I'm an Android girl!), it will "download" and then "store" certain programs—pushing them into the "background" so that the more important "programs" can be running up front. New things or challenging things that you are doing or learning are the main focus of your brain, but in order for you to be able to do them, it has to put certain other programs on hold.

The brain likes to push different activities, habits, and even thoughts into the background, so that you are more efficient and thus can do more things at once. For instance, as a young child, it took every ounce of your concentration to walk without falling over. Now, you can probably walk, talk, chew gum, think about school, and text with your friends, all at the same time. Some of those things get pushed into the background (walking and chewing) so that your active brain—the conscious stuff—can be used for the more complicated stuff that you're actually doing.

But we *also* have to know how to bring up old programs and change them if they aren't running properly. Think of your computer—when your system starts running really slowly, and you hit Ctrl-Alt-Delete to bring up the task manager, you see all these other programs running in the background of your computer that you maybe had no idea were running at all. You can then open those programs, change them, or close them if they aren't helping the system anymore. In the same way, when we have certain habits that we have learned and then stored in the background of our mind, we have to be able to slow down, pull them back out, and take the time to change them around again.

let's try it

Step 1)   I want you to just cross your arms for a second. Don't think about it too much, just go ahead and cross them over your chest like you might if you were cold, or relaxed in a conversation.

Step 2)   Just briefly look down and notice which arm rests on top. Once you note this, uncross your arms and check off which arm was on top:

☐ Left   ☐ Right

Step 3)   Now that you've got that, shake your arms out for a second. Now, I want you to cross them again—but this time the other way. That's right. Cross your arms the *opposite way* from what you did before, so that the arm that was on top is now on the bottom, and vice versa. Once you have done this, hold that position for a minute or two.

Which was harder—the first time or the second time? _____

What happened when you tried to do it the opposite way?

_____

_____

How did it feel to hold the opposite position of crossing your arms?

_____

_____

What you just noticed was your brain resisting change—involving something as simple as crossing your arms in a certain way, which you probably do all the time. Your brain has decided that the way you do it already is fine, so there is no point in learning to do it another way. Your brain wants to keep you running at peak efficiency, so it doesn't want you to change something unless there's a really good reason for it to change.

What this means is that when you want to change something in your life that you have been doing a certain way for a long time (including thinking in a certain way), your brain usually tells you that changing it is not right—that it's phony, fake, or weird. The fact that your brain does this is actually totally normal, even though it may be uncomfortable! This means that your brain is working properly. Keep pushing. If you keep doing it, practicing it, and leaning into that discomfort, over time you can help your brain to form new habits, new pathways, and new skills. You *do* have the power to change your story and to adapt to new things—you just have to help your brain trust that some particular change is really important, and to push through that initial resistance.

Over the next week or two, try to cross your arms the other way every time you remember and see if it gets easier. It should! Your brain will start to get more flexible the more you do it.

Every now and then, some people find that arm-crossing exercise really easy. If you happen to be one of those people, this may be a more challenging exercise: Try writing your name with your opposite hand!

more to try

The same thing that our brain does with physical things that we learn (crossing our arms, writing our name, how we walk and talk, etc.) it also does with our thoughts. Our brains are set up to take in information, then store it, and then move on to the next thing. This is great! At least…it's great until we want to go back and grab something we learned, pull it out of the system, and change it. Our brains don't like that. If that was super easy to do—if we could just pull out any piece of information and undo it on any given whim with little or no effort—the system would become pretty unreliable and unstable. So our brains make it more difficult, to make sure that we *really* want to make that change.

Think of it like building a house of cards. Each new card you put into your house takes a lot of focus and effort. And each card needs a few other cards to rely on to stand in place. (Every thought and fact has to be related to another fact in some way to make sense to us as well.) Once a card is in place in that house just right, that card stays pretty stable, and you can keep building on top of it. But if you wanted to go back and pull a card out, a whole bunch of cards often come with it. So this house of cards wants you to be *really sure* you want to change something, because it will take a lot of energy to make that happen. So it's going to put up a whole lot of roadblocks in your way before it's going to let you actually pull a card out of that house and change it around.

Let's see this system in action. Here's an exercise to show you what this is like for the brain and the house of cards it is building.

Okay, so first things first. This question may sound a little weird, but without overthinking it too much, just answer the question below as to what your first instinct is, and write it in the space below. Ready?

Picture two items, or find them in the room you're in: a clock and a tissue box.

Between the two items—the clock and the tissue box—which one is better?

_____

Why? List a few reasons that you come up with here.

_____

_____

_____

_____

Okay, now write down some reasons why the *other item* (the one that you didn't initially choose between the clock and the tissue box)—is actually the better item.

_____

_____

_____

_____

Which question was easier to answer?

1. Listing the reasons the item you first chose was "better."

2. Listing the reasons the *opposite* item than you chose was "better."

So now let's stop and think for a second.

Do you think there is a true "right" answer to this question? When we stop and think, there really isn't. Either item could be considered "better"—it all depends on how you look at it or what you compare it to. The trouble is, once your brain has decided on one thing, your brain doesn't like to change from that decision.

Even though, *logically*, we know there is no "right" answer to this, I want you to notice if your brain echoes back to you anyway and says, "Well, maybe not, but my answer was still the best." Often, the brain keeps chiming in on the decision it made, trying to shore up that house of cards and put some roadblocks in your way before it lets you truly release that arbitrary belief you just made up in your head right now.

The point here is this: As we develop ideas or decisions about how life is and why it is the way that it is, we create another little card in our "worldview"—the way we see and interpret the world around us. Most of these little cards get put into our house and they work just fine. Most people agree on most things at a basic level. No one would argue against the fact that a microwave oven is larger than a pen, for instance. Most physical things in the world around us are largely agreed upon.

But when it comes to values, to meaning, to identity, and to purpose in our lives, things really do become more up to whoever is writing the script. The good news is, you get to write your own script. Even though it doesn't always feel like it, the first step is learning that you *can* take charge of that script, and even if something has felt "written in stone" for years and years, you can unwrite it. You can unpublish that story in your brain and replace it with a new one. Or you can add a new chapter. We are going to explore this more in the next activity.

It might feel like your house of cards is going to tumble down when you try this—but sometimes this little internal crumbling of an old or unhelpful idea is a *good* thing. You then get to change and rebuild that part of your house of cards in a way that works for *you*.

2 storytelling and perspectives

let's get started

The way we think about things has a big effect on how we get through things. One of the important things to recognize in life is that there is no singular reality—there is no singular truth. In each and every thing that we experience, how we see and experience events depends a lot on *us* and how we choose to interpret life events. We are the writers of our own story.

When we experience something in life, we tend to write a little script in our heads—a "narrative" of how our life is going, what is going on around us, and how events are playing out. We all do this! We have a little movie and a little playback button we can hit when we scroll backward into memories. This background voice (like the movie-guy voice that does all the movie trailers) can also impact how we will interpret *future* events as well.

The trouble here is that most of us have our movie-guy (or girl) voice in our heads that has been talking along our whole lives, but we've never really paid much attention to that voice. And we never really stop to consider that that voice is one that we actually have control over—it's not just on autoplay (or at least it shouldn't be!). This voice is incredibly important—and we are going to get to know it better through this book.

This internal voice and this way of looking at things is something that we actually *do* have some control over! We may not be able to choose all of the events that happen to us in our lives, but we can choose how we write our own scripts.

let's try it

I want you to think of this classic story—this story that everyone knows—"Romeo and Juliet." Your job right now is to write the story from the perspective of someone who *loves* the story and thinks it is the greatest love story ever told.

_____

_____

_____

_____

_____

_____

Okay, now your job is to write the story from the perspective of someone who thinks that Romeo and Juliet were being "ridiculous teenagers," and that it is an incredibly immature story.

_____

_____

_____

_____

_____

_____

Notice how the story itself didn't change, but that the way you told the story changed how you felt about what happened. And that you had the power to change the story— just by changing how you described the events.

You can also try this again with other stories that you know well—try "Cinderella," or "Snow White," or "The Three Little Pigs."

more to try

So how do you know which story is "right"? This leads us now to a much larger conversation. You see, the brain doesn't like to live in uncertainty. It likes to *decide*. This is because it takes more energy to live in a state of uncertainty, and your body tries to conserve energy wherever it can. So your brain looks at the information that it has at the time, then it writes a story, then it stores that story in the background and keeps going.

The flaw in the design of the brain is that when we write our stories too quickly, or when we decide something at a certain time in our lives without ever revisiting or challenging that story, we may end up with a belief that does not allow us to grow, expand, or change.

There's a very simple four-step method based on CBT for recognizing and challenging those negative stories (inspired by Greenberger & Padesky, 2015). For an example, let's look at how Austin deals with this type of challenge of a "stuck" narrative.

Step 1: Identify the Stuck Thought

Austin: I'm bad at public speaking.

Step 2: Evidence Supporting the Stuck Thought

Austin: I shake like a leaf and my mouth gets dry and I need every word written down or I screw up when I'm public speaking.

Step 3: Evidence Against the Stuck Thought

Austin: I guess I do usually get good marks when I give presentations, and teachers keep encouraging me to trust myself more. That must mean something. And I had that one awesome experience recently of being able to talk freely as soon as I trusted myself that I knew what I was talking about and didn't use so many notes.

Step 4: Replace the Stuck Thought with a More Balanced Thought

Austin: If I don't trust myself or if I make too many notes, I can make myself nervous and this makes me not perform well. If I trust myself and allow myself to speak from the heart, I actually can speak quite well in front of groups, even if I'm nervous!

Okay, reader, now it's your turn!

Step 1: Identify the Stuck Thought

Write down something you're currently struggling with, something you wish was different. Maybe your brain has told you that you aren't good at art, that you aren't very smart, that you are awkward, or that you aren't attractive.

_____

Step 2: Evidence Supporting the Stuck Thought

Why do you think this? What evidence do you have that this story is true—that is, what happened that caused your brain to write that story?

_____

_____

_____

Step 3: Evidence Against the Stuck Thought

Now, think of a time when maybe that story wasn't 100% true. Maybe a time you made some art you were pretty happy with, even if it wasn't the best in the world; or maybe a time you got a hard question on a test right, or that you made a new friend at a camp or event, or that a boy or girl showed some interest in you or complimented you on something. This is going to ask your brain to stretch itself outside of the story line that it finds more comfortable—and it's going to resist that change! Remember, that's normal. In fact, that's exactly the feeling we are looking for!

_____

_____

_____

_____

_____

Step 4: Replace the Stuck Thought with a More Balanced Thought

Now that you have some evidence *for* the old story (in support of it), but you also have some evidence *against* the old story (why it might not be 100% true), try writing a story that's a bit more balanced. Try to use words like "sometimes," "often," "in some cases," "maybe," and other qualifiers that leave room for change and growth in the story. Avoid using words like "worst" or "always" or "never" when used in the negative sense, or negative labels like "bad," "awful," "loser," and so on.

_____

_____

_____

_____

_____

Awesome! This four-step process is one that you can use at any time when you find yourself stuck in a narrative or a story about yourself or your life that is holding you back, stealing your confidence, or limiting your ability to change, grow, and learn.

letting go of your old story 3

let's get started

Any time you rewrite a story, there's a catch. Let's say you want to leave an unpleasant relationship you are in. Your story will change. Your life will change. Or let's say you learn to manage anxiety and it no longer impacts your everyday life—who will you be then? How will you define yourself?

Big changes can often be hard to make and hard to think about—even positive changes can feel scary, because what does life look like on the "other side"? It can feel like jumping off a high diving board without being able to see the pool below you. You have to just jump and free fall and hope that something is there to catch you. This is one of the big reasons why people often stay stuck in old stories and old patterns even when a part of them wants to change—because at least those old stories are predictable and familiar. At least you know what struggles you will face.

It can also feel super hard to say goodbye to an old story, because you may also have gained something from that old part of yourself. In fact, sometimes we actually have to grieve for the loss of part of ourselves as we say goodbye and welcome change. We often have a relationship developed with an old story. It feels familiar. It may not be a perfect story, but it's your story. If you change that story, does that mean you're not "you" anymore? If you let go of a part of your story, does it just leave a vacuum behind?

So when we look at changing a story, we also have to think about saying goodbye to that old story and looking ahead to what that new space in our lives can become. This is one of the most important parts of adapting to change—recognizing that while change can be good, there's almost always a small part of us that has to grieve for the loss of something else as we shift into the new.

let's try it

In life we have to grieve when things change, no matter what they may be. For instance, we may have had our heart set on getting into a certain program at school, or on dating a certain person, or on having a certain kind of relationship with our siblings or our friends. The process is very similar to how we actually grieve for the loss of loved ones or pets that may have passed away and that we have to say goodbye to. We have to name the thing we are grieving for, and then we need a formal processing of that loss—the same way we have a formal way of processing someone's passing away with a funeral or other ritual to honor that person and what they meant to us.

Take a separate piece of paper, then write out and process something that you are upset about because it didn't work out the way you hoped. It may be a real tangible thing that you lost, or it may be the idea, the hope, or the dream of how something was supposed to be that didn't turn out the way you wanted it to. Then write down answers to the following questions:

What are you grieving the loss of—what hasn't worked out, or what are you upset about that hasn't been the way you dreamed it would be?

What emotions do you feel when you think about this?

Where in your body do you feel those emotions? (Tight in throat, heavy in chest, tense in back, etc.)

Take a moment, close your eyes, and breathe deeply in and out while you notice those thoughts, emotions, and feelings in your body. Take your time. Just let whatever happens, happen. It can help to gently tap your toes back and forth on the floor or in your shoes while you think about this to help keep you grounded and to help you process your thoughts—a processing approach from EMDR (Shapiro, 2013).

Next, I want you to take that piece of paper and think of something that feels meaningful to do as a release ritual. It may be taking it to a safe space and slowly ripping it into pieces as you say goodbye. It may be taking it to a safe place and folding it away, or closing it in a book, like a chapter closing behind you. It may be going for a walk in a park and tossing it into a trashcan by the water or somewhere far away from your home. It may be painting a picture on top of what you have written, covering it up and creating something new from these words. It may be folding it into an origami shape that is meaningful to you and putting it on a shelf somewhere. It may be tucking it into a memory jar that you make, paint, or create, and storing it safely somewhere. Pick a ritual that is meaningful to you and allow this memory, idea, or thought to be released as you grieve for its loss, and allow yourself to process that. Breathe deeply as you do all of this.

Lean into the difficult emotions, feel your feelings, and validate for yourself that it is normal and okay to grieve for the things in life that didn't work out the way that you hoped. It is through grieving for these losses that you can create space for the next part of your story.

more to try

While we have things in our life that we have to say goodbye to in order to make room for the new things and to move into the next stage of our lives, we also have parts inside ourselves that we may want to change—and these parts need a similar goodbye process as well if they are going to shift and change (Schwartz, 1997).

I want you to think of a part of yourself that you've been struggling with. Maybe it is low self-esteem, anxiety, explosive anger, a gossipy part of yourself, an easily hurt part of yourself, a way of viewing yourself. Describe this part of yourself below.

_____

_____

_____

What name can you give this part of yourself? (For example, "Angry Part" or "Gossipy Part.")

_____

What do you think this part of you has been trying to do to help your overall self? (For example, "The Angry Part of me has tried to protect me from being hurt by other people," or "The Gossipy Part of me has tried to help me make friends and be interesting and liked.")

_____

_____

_____

What do you think this part might be afraid of if it steps back or changes? (For example, that you'll get hurt more easily, or that people might not like you as much.)

_____

_____

What can you tell this part of yourself to reassure it that you can handle those fears that might happen? (For example, people might hurt you more easily if you're not as angry, but you have other parts of yourself that can cope with that hurt, and you have people you can talk to in order to work through it.)

_____

_____

If you were to tell this part of yourself that it doesn't have to work so hard anymore, that there are other parts of you that can help, and that this part can step back and give you more room—does that part feel like it is ready to let you do that?

☐ Yes ☐ No

If not—what does this part feel like it still needs you to know?

_____

_____

Depending on what you may have written above, see if there is a way you can reassure this part of yourself about what might be missing.

If this part is ready to step back and give you more room to make new choices and try new things—what role could this part of you do instead? (For example, could Angry Part maybe just be an internal "tap on the shoulder" to let you know when someone might be crossing a boundary with you? Could Gossipy Part use her bubbly or excited energy to connect with friends in a different way, through a different kind of humor?)

_____

_____

Thank this part of you for doing the job it has been doing so far, and thank it for being willing to try to make new changes and work with you in a different way from now on.

_____

_____

Now that you and that "part" are on the same side, think of the grieving exercise we just did and how it might apply to saying goodbye to the things in your life that this part might have brought to you. For instance, you might have to say goodbye to the excitement that the Gossipy Part brought to your life, even though you knew it wasn't good for you in the long term. You might have to say goodbye to the power that the Angry Part made you feel in a moment of intense emotion, even though it was hurting your relationships in the big picture. Do the same exercise here with saying goodbye that you did in the previous exercise to help you open up to the next step of changing your story and your narrative. Write what you will do below.

_____

_____

_____

_____

Goal 2

Overcoming Adversity

4 understanding stress

let's get started

Let's be honest: stress can be a very uncomfortable experience. In fact, that's kind of stress's job—to make you uncomfortable. Stress sends signals to the body that something is not quite right, that something needs to be done, changed, or fixed. At extremes, such as with high levels of anxiety, stress is your body's warning system that it might be in mortal danger and that it should run, fight, or freeze, as the case requires, so that you may live to see another day. Our body has a whole host of biological processes it triggers almost instantaneously when a threat is detected. Sometimes our system responds before we even know what set us off!

A lot of these changes in our body are important to keep us safe, and therefore many of them are a bit uncomfortable, physically. This physical discomfort makes us aware and alert to what's going on around us—it can wake us from a sleepy or relaxed state and put our brains and bodies into the next gear, in case we have to act quickly. This is great for times we literally walk into danger, like exploring a cave and finding a bear inside. That kind of stress would make sure we go out safely—and really quickly!

So stress has two roles: it sends us signals to get out or get away from the thing causing us stress, while at the same time making us more alert, more efficient, and more effective to do whatever it is that needs to be done in order to make the stress go away.

This leaves us with a fun little "stress curve" (Diamond et al., 2007):

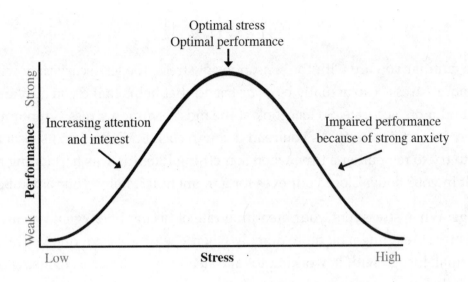

What this shows us is that with too little stress, we actually don't function very efficiently at all. Think of the last project you had to do for school that was due more than a month away. You likely didn't worry too much about it at that point, right? There wasn't enough stress to get your body really geared up to function yet. Then, there was likely the "sweet spot," maybe one or two weeks out, where your body and mind realized—*It's go time!* Time to get working on this, it's due soon. If you happened to miss that "sweet spot" window, you might have gone up and over the top of this curve, until you panicked, froze, and instead binge-watched Netflix for a bit to distract yourself from the discomfort, and then eventually pulled an all-nighter or two to get it done—if you were still able to do it at all after that point.

What this graph shows us is that we actually *do* need some stress to perform at our best! The viral TED Talk by stress researcher and author Kelly McGonigal, "How to Make Stress Your Friend," says this quite clearly. A bit of stress is natural and healthy, and even if it's a bit uncomfortable, it actually puts us in that "sweet spot" zone at the top of the curve. Olympic athletes, for instance, spend a lot of time learning to harness that sweet spot of stress…they know they need those stress responses to perform at their best, and they practice getting very familiar with the body sensations that come with it. They make those sensations familiar old friends. Let's do the same here!

let's try it

The more familiar you are with the sensations of stress, the less scary they will be and the more "stress" can actually be your friend that helps make you stronger, more efficient, and more accurate. So let's look at the most common stress symptoms, and where they impact our body. As you read through each body part and sensation, take a moment to try to remember a time when something like this was happening to you, and how it felt in your body. Close your eyes for a moment if it helps you remember.

Your lungs: When stress hits, your breathing rate of taking in oxygen increases. If you feel like you're breathing a bit more quickly when you're stressed, don't be alarmed! That's normal. Just go with it, working to take steady, deep breaths, focusing on a long exhale to help keep yourself in "the zone."

Your heart: Your heart rate usually kicks up a few notches when you're feeling stress. This is perfectly normal—just keep breathing and don't panic about the strange feeling. It's just part of your body getting ready for the next task at hand!

Your skin: Especially your palms, underarms, and anywhere else that comes to mind when you think of sweat! This is your body's cooling system. It turns on to help keep your body ready to run or fight even longer without overheating. It's normal and healthy. Just load up on the antiperspirant in the morning and wear patterns or the color black if this happens to you more often—and then keep on going!

Your stomach: When you get stressed, your body has to make a moment-to-moment decision. It only has a limited amount of energy, so it decides that if something is threatening, it's going to redirect all of its energy toward helping you run for longer or fight for longer, if necessary. It does this by pushing "pause" on any nonessential body functions, the main one being digestion. So if you find yourself feeling a bit nauseated when you're stressed, it's because your digestion actually has been put on hold, and so the food that's in there can feel like a bit of an uncomfortable lump. Just remember that this sensation is temporary, and you're not actually sick!

Your eyes: Your eyes will dilate when you're stressed, and sometimes you can find yourself a bit sensitive to light.

Your muscles: When your body goes into its stress response, it really, really wants you to move your body in some way. When you try to hold your body still, it sends signals to the muscle-twitch fibers that make your muscles expand and contract, telling them that you should really be moving now, which sometimes ends up making you just shake on the spot. This is normal, too. Move around a bit if you can—this can calm down the shaking because you're putting those muscles to work!

more to do

Think about your own personal sensations when you are stressed or anxious. Which sensations do you feel the most strongly? Write them down here.

_____

_____

If these sensations feel worrying in any way, write down any fears that you may have about these types of sensations. (If you feel it would be helpful, you can also check in with a trusted adult or even your doctor about these fears, to help your brain feel like it can trust your body more when it pops up into a stress response.)

_____

_____

Now that you know about the normal body responses and sensations that happen with stress, what can you tell yourself about the above-mentioned fears of those responses and sensations when they show up, even if they are uncomfortable? (For example, I might feel like I have to throw up, but I know that feeling is actually normal and doesn't mean "I'm sick".)

_____

_____

Now, take a moment to remember a thrilling experience you have had in your life. Maybe it was playing a sport, going on a roller coaster, seeing a scary movie, or jumping off a high diving board. Think for a moment what it felt like during this thrilling experience. Write it down here.

_____

_____

_____

What body sensations did you notice while this experience was happening?

_____

_____

_____

Interestingly, the same body sensations that you get with stress are happening with something thrilling. The same adrenaline and other hormones are being released—the big difference is your _interpretation_ of the situation and sensations. What were you telling yourself during this thrilling adventure? What made it feel fun for you?

_____

_____

_____

The next time you feel those sensations with something that you may have previously felt intimidated by (public speaking, performing, writing a test, etc.), remember that you had those same sensations other times in your life when you were having fun (for example, riding a roller coaster). What can you tell yourself, in your own words, to help make stress your friend in those situations, too? (For example, "These sensations may be uncomfortable, but it just means that my body is preparing for the next task at hand—it's helping me!") Write yours below.

_____

_____

5 grit and growth mindset

let's get started

There's a lot of emphasis in our world on things like IQ and talent—everyone is quick to point out people who are immediately good or talented at something. If we try something in life, such as a new sport or hobby, and we aren't immediately rock stars at it…should we just assume that we are subpar and stop doing something we clearly aren't "gifted" at?

The true measure of success is not talent, not IQ, and not inborn or innate abilities—it's having passion and perseverance for long-term goals, having stamina, and sticking with your future. This is known as "grit" (Duckworth et al., 2007).

The ability to have and develop grit has a lot to do with the last section's goals. So far, we have learned how to challenge the brain, and we've learned about the "turn back now!" signals the brain sends us to preserve its efficiency (it wants you to be *really* sure about changing the wiring it put a lot of energy into creating before it lets you do it). We've learned that sometimes even the beliefs we have that *feel* like undeniable facts may, on closer inspection, be somewhat arbitrary and changeable with a bit of effort. This includes our beliefs about ourselves, and our own stories and identities as well.

One of the biggest components of grit is called "growth mindset" (Yeager & Dweck, 2012). This is the belief that the ability to learn is not fixed, but that it can change with the amount of effort you put in, and that intelligence can be developed through effort. This is in contrast to a "fixed mindset"—which is the belief that intelligence is static and that skills, talents, and abilities are mostly inborn and unchangeable. You can develop your growth-mindset skills. Remember, you are in charge of your own story.

let's try it

Where are you starting from? Circle True (T) or False (F) for the following questions:

1. If I'm not good at something right away, I tend to stop that activity fairly quickly.

    T   F

2. If I receive criticism about something I am doing, it means that I'm not good enough at it.

    T   F

3. I believe I was born smart or not smart—that's just the way it is.

    T   F

4. When friends of mine are better at a new activity or task than I am right away, I feel stupid.

    T   F

5. When I am trying to learn something new and I make mistakes, I feel like a failure.

    T   F

6. If I have to put a lot of effort into something, it means I'm not good enough or smart enough at it—things should come to you easily if you're smart or talented.

    T   F

7. If I answer a question wrong in class, I believe I look stupid for getting it wrong—questions should only be answered if I am 100% sure I am right.

    T   F

8. My brain can only think in certain ways and only do certain things—it's not going to change.

    T   F

Okay, have a look at your T/F ratio—how many T's did you have? It's okay if you had some, because that's what we are tackling in this workbook! But those are the places we want to help your brain stretch. We want to challenge those beliefs and storylines, like we learned in the previous chapter.

If you circled any "T's" in the above list, think about the following questions about them:

How old were you when you first learned those ideas or developed those beliefs?

_____

Was there an influential person, or situation that happened, when you first "downloaded" and adopted those ways of thinking?

_____

On a scale of 1 to 10, with 10 being "yes, completely!" and 1 being "not a chance, never"—how willing are you to try to stretch your brain to look at new ways of thinking and believing and change those T's to F's?

   1   2   3   4   5   6   7   8   9   10

Look at the number you chose—if it's more than 1 and less than 10—I want you to think and write down: Why didn't you pick the number below it? (For example, if you picked 5, why didn't you pick 4?)

_____

_____

If you picked a 1, what do you feel needs to change in your life or what do you feel you need to do to make that 1 become a 2? Whatever you write here below, think about talking to a trusted adult about it to see if they can help you in this area.

_____

_____

_____

Read the following ideas and let your mind consider them. On the 1 to 10 scale below each sentence, indicate how much you currently believe each statement, and on the 1 to 10 scale below that, how much you'd *like* to believe that statement.

1. If I'm not good at something right away, that's normal! Everyone has to start somewhere, and even the greatest experts, at one point in their life, also started out knowing nothing.

   How much do you currently believe this? (1 = not at all, 10 = totally!)

   1   2   3   4   5   6   7   8   9   10

   How much would you *like* to believe this? (1 = not at all, 10 = totally!)

   1   2   3   4   5   6   7   8   9   10

2. If I receive criticism about something I am doing, it gives me a chance to improve and to do even better next time. It doesn't mean I'm not good enough—it means I'm still learning, which is a good thing. Every single one of us is always learning, every day, no matter how good we get at certain things! Even experts and adults of all ages.

   How much do you currently believe this? (1 = not at all, 10 = totally!)

   1   2   3   4   5   6   7   8   9   10

   How much would you *like* to believe this? (1 = not at all, 10 = totally!)

   1   2   3   4   5   6   7   8   9   10

3. I believe I was born with certain skills and abilities—and that every single one of those can be built and developed and changed and improved with practice and with effort.

   How much do you currently believe this? (1 = not at all, 10 = totally!)

   1   2   3   4   5   6   7   8   9   10

How much would you *like* to believe this? (1 = not at all, 10 = totally!)

1   2   3   4   5   6   7   8   9   10

4. Even if friends of mine are better at a new activity or task than I am right away, I feel confident that I can continue to learn and grow as well, with effort and practice, and that the end result of my or my friend's skills and abilities has more to do with ongoing effort than it does with whatever "original" talent we may have started out with.

How much do you currently believe this? (1 = not at all, 10 = totally!)

1   2   3   4   5   6   7   8   9   10

How much would you *like* to believe this? (1 = not at all, 10 = totally!)

1   2   3   4   5   6   7   8   9   10

5. When I am trying to learn something new and I make mistakes, that is actually a good thing—this is where real learning happens! Making mistakes is how I learn to do better in the future.

How much do you currently believe this? (1 = not at all, 10 = totally!)

1   2   3   4   5   6   7   8   9   10

How much would you *like* to believe this? (1 = not at all, 10 = totally!)

1   2   3   4   5   6   7   8   9   10

6. If I have to put a lot of effort into something, that means I'll continue to get better the more I practice. Sometimes different things may take more effort for different people, but the more I work at something, the better I'll get!

How much do you currently believe this? (1 = not at all, 10 = totally!)

1   2   3   4   5   6   7   8   9   10

How much would you *like* to believe this? (1 = not at all, 10 = totally!)

1   2   3   4   5   6   7   8   9   10

7. If I answer a question wrong in class, that's going to help me remember the answer better for the test later on in the class—and that's where the real marks come from! Trying to answer a question is a huge part of learning and remembering information.

How much do you currently believe this? (1 = not at all, 10 = totally!)

1   2   3   4   5   6   7   8   9   10

How much would you *like* to believe this? (1 = not at all, 10 = totally!)

1   2   3   4   5   6   7   8   9   10

8. My brain is constantly growing, changing, and evolving—I have the skill and capability to continue learning, growing, and developing throughout my entire life.

How much do you currently believe this? (1 = not at all, 10 = totally!)

1   2   3   4   5   6   7   8   9   10

How much would you *like* to believe this? (1 = not at all, 10 = totally!)

1   2   3   4   5   6   7   8   9   10

For any of the scales you just answered, where your "current belief" score was lower than your "*like* to believe" score, jot down a few ideas you might have on how you can continue to work to stretch your brain on that particular idea, any thoughts you might have on where you are getting stuck, or other reflections you had pop up as you answered the above questions. And don't worry—throughout the rest of the book, we'll continue to build new ideas and skills to help you achieve your goals that you've set out here as well!

_____

_____

_____

_____

_____

more to try

It also helps to stretch your brain into a growth mindset with a few simple key words and phrases. First, we want to avoid these two key words in our life if used in a negative way—"**always**" and "**never**." Next, we want to add in some amazingly powerful words and phrases to our vocabulary. These are called "qualifiers" and they are our new best friends. Some examples of these are:

Yet—Often—Sometimes—Every Now and Then—Somewhat—Maybe—So Far—Right Now—In Some Cases

Often when we are struggling with something or finding something difficult in life, we may switch to an "all-or-nothing" brain. This is the version of our brain that tells us things like "I'm terrible at writing essays" or "I can't play basketball" or "I always get low grades in math." Notice how these sentences can leave us feeling like, "Well, that's that, and there's nothing to be done about it!" We get stuck and can feel hopeless, and this can make us give up and stop trying. And of all the things in life, giving up is one of the only guaranteed ways that things *won't* get better!

We want your brain to realize that change is always possible, that things can always be practiced, and that skills can always be developed. Nothing is set in stone! Let's try those sentences again with some qualifiers around them to open them back up to changing and reempowering ourselves, even if things are a bit challenging or difficult right now. There are three simple rules to this process:

1. Avoid the use of "**always**" and "**never**" if used in a negative way—cut it out!

2. Add in a qualifier to help you open up to change and possibility.

3. Add in a "**but**" and describe how you can change and grow, even if things are hard right now.

Let's see this in action:

*   "I'm terrible at writing essays." Change it to: "I'm terrible at writing essays *so far* (qualifier)…**but** I can get better if I keep practicing!"

- "I can't play basketball." Change it to: "I can't play basketball *yet* (qualifier)…**but** if I start practicing I can learn how!"

- "I always get low grades in math." Change it to: "I get low grades in math *right now* (qualifier)…**but** I can get better if I work with a tutor!"

Try a few of your own below.

What's a challenging or negative thought you are currently struggling with?

_____

_____

Now rewrite it here, using those three rules above.

_____

_____

Try a few more below!

_____

_____

_____

_____

_____

_____

distress tolerance: the ice cube experiment 6

We are often taught that life should always be happy, pleasant, or fair—but as I'm sure you're noticing in your life that unfortunately isn't always the case. But it is truly through our struggles that we find our strength. In any good movie, the main character has to have some kind of obstacle or conflict, and struggle through it, and then find a way to overcome it, right? Harry Potter couldn't have been Harry Potter without losing his parents and without Voldemort (sorry, He-Who-Must-Not-Be-Named!), and Cinderella couldn't have been Cinderella without her Evil Stepmother. So while difficult times in life hurt, sting, and break our hearts, those are the same moments that you *can* get through, tolerate, and overcome, and that can bring you strength—as long as you face them.

Your ability to handle and tolerate difficult emotions is something that you can grow and develop, similarly to how you can learn to tolerate physical discomfort. Think of a difficult physical obstacle you have gone through in your life. Maybe you have trained in a sport. Maybe you have learned to lift progressively heavier weights. Maybe you have walked or run progressively longer distances. Each time, you pushed through a challenging feeling and kept going. You can do the same thing with your emotional sensations, thoughts, or feelings.

What makes this tolerance a bit more challenging with emotions, however, is that our brain has borrowed the same circuitry for physical pain as it uses for emotional pain (Eisenberger, Lieberman, & Williams, 2003). This means that, just like when you get your foot stepped on and your natural inclination is to get out from under that pain, we get these same intense signals of "change something!" with emotional pain. This can be a problem for us, and it can sometimes make us feel helpless and overwhelmed because there are so many emotional things in life that we can't change right away, or maybe not even at all. We can't make our parents not get a divorce. We can't bring someone back who has passed away. We can't make a boy or girl like us back romantically if they're not interested. We can't undo something embarrassing that has already happened.

So it's important to get to know your normal reactions to uncomfortable physical pain, and then recognize when those same reactions come up with emotional pain. Then we can learn to apply the skill of distress tolerance for the times when we can't change our situation right away, or even not at all (McKay, 2007). Instead, we need to tolerate and allow the pain or discomfort as we work through it, grieve over it, and process it. As we do this, our brains will strengthen and our ability to sit with those feelings will increase, just like with physical strength. And slowly the pain will lessen as our strength and resilience grow.

Let's look at Casey's story.

Casey had been feeling really low lately. He was often upset, tossed and turned about by so many difficult things in his life to this point. By ninth grade he'd already had his best friend move away, been turned down by the girl he had had a crush on for years, and had gone through his parent's challenging and chaotic divorce. When he was alone in his room, he often would get overwhelmed with thoughts of sadness—and hating this uncomfortable feeling, he would do everything he could to ignore the thoughts and just stay busy instead. But it didn't always work. His inner thoughts would rush forward, "I can't do this. This hurts too much. This is more than I can bear. I don't know what to do. I'm not strong enough to get through this."

Casey knew there must be another way to get through these feelings—so he found out about the skill of distress tolerance.

Casey learned that, the same way that he was able to push himself in hockey practice until his legs burned and sweat dripped in his eyes and his whole body ached, he could use those same skills of tolerating physical pain and exertion to tolerate his emotional pain and challenges, too. He realized that he could use the same inner voice and the same recovery skills that he did when he was exhausted from hockey to keep going and pushing through.

He learned that if he was supportive and compassionate with himself, and accepting of the difficult emotions, the same way he was able to be accepting of the ache in his legs from hockey practice, that he could get through the intense feelings and still be okay after riding the wave of emotions. He learned that the ebb and flow of difficult emotions also made the joys of life more vibrant and meaningful for him as well. He learned that it is, in fact, a skill to be able to be upset and to feel intense emotions, and like any skill, it was one that he could learn. And only through feeling his emotions was he able to work through them; to grieve for them, heal from them, and then rebuild and move forward with the next stage of his life.

let's try it

For this exercise we are going to activate that fight-or-flight side of your brain—the same part that is activated when you experience unpleasant emotions. It's the same part of the brain that comes up with physical discomfort as it does with emotional discomfort. Let's get to know it better so that you can map some of the skills you already have and then tap into them, grow them, and develop them, in order to manage the emotional side of your brain, too.

For this exercise you need three things:

1. An ice cube

2. A bowl

3. A timer

Take the ice cube and put it in the bowl. Now with one hand, get ready to grab the ice cube, and with the other, get ready to start the timer. You're going to hold on to the ice cube as long as you can, and while doing it, track what happens in your brain as you do it. If you have to let go at any time, notice—what was the last thing you said to yourself before you let go? On three, grab the ice cube and squeeze and start the timer!

One…two…three…go!

How long did you make it for? Record your time here: _____

What kinds of things did your brain start doing or saying to you when you first grabbed that ice cube?

_____

_____

What kinds of things did your brain start saying as you kept going?

_____

_____

What kinds of things did your brain start saying if or when you had to let go?

_____

_____

Okay, once your hand has warmed up and feels back to normal, I want you to try it again. If for any reason that felt super easy to you, you can also try the "expert level" version: Grab a juice jug and fill it with one-third ice cubes and the rest of the way up with water, leaving enough volume space to submerge—yes—your whole forearm into the water. Try the timer again with this "expert level" option if you want to up your game!

Let's try again. Start that timer! See if you can make it longer than last time.

How long did you make it this time? Record your time here: _____

If you were able to make it longer than last time, what was different?

_____

_____

If you were able to make it longer than last time, what did you tell yourself in your head in order to be able to do that?

_____

_____

If you weren't able to do it longer than last time, what can you try to help yourself make it a little bit longer next time? Perhaps some encouraging things you can say to yourself, or borrowing a skill in another area of your life to apply here to this exercise?

_____

_____

The skill here is to notice the types of things your brain does that make you want to stop doing something that is unpleasant. This is very important because this is where the ways of dealing with emotional pain and physical pain differ. Often, we can change our environment or situation quite quickly with physical pain or discomfort. If we are hot, we can take off a sweater. If we are cold, we can turn up the heat. Our brain sends us the signal of "change something!" when we are uncomfortable physically, because those changes can keep us alive (so we don't freeze to death, and so on).

However, with emotional pain, we actually have to tolerate those sensations, sit with the discomfort as we process it (sometimes, doing this in small windows of time instead of all at once is important, so we don't get overwhelmed), grieve for the loss or pain, and then eventually heal from it. So we have to know how to recognize those "change something!" signals that make us try to avoid the sensations and feelings, and learn instead how to lean into those uncomfortable feelings, allow them, accept them, and support ourselves through them (like holding on to the ice cube for longer and longer).

more to try

I want you to imagine something challenging in your own life that you will have to face soon. A test you have to complete, a difficult conversation with someone you are worried about, or something else.

Now imagine the emotion that you are anticipating that will feel the most uncomfortable. What is that emotion?

_____

Can you remember another time in your life when you have felt that emotion before and have gotten through that experience? Write that memory down here.

_____

_____

What did you say to yourself to manage and tolerate that difficult emotion in the past?

_____

_____

What are other ways that you can add in to help yourself tolerate that difficult emotion coming up in your life soon? Perhaps include here some of the things that you used to encourage yourself to get through the discomfort of holding on to that ice cube. Write what that might sound like below—what you can say to yourself in your head to help you get through and tolerate the discomfort.

_____

_____

_____

direct discomfort versus indirect discomfort 7

While we are practicing our distress tolerance, sometimes we can fall into a trap of spiraling into other related memories of distress or discomfort. This can make our pain bigger than it really needs to be at the time. This is the difference between "direct discomfort" and "indirect discomfort" (also sometimes referred to as "clean" discomfort versus "dirty" discomfort—but we will use "direct" and "indirect" here for clarity). Basically, we want to allow ourselves to experience and tolerate *direct discomfort*, but we also want to keep our brains from spiraling into *indirect discomfort* instead. Let's look at what those two terms mean.

Direct discomfort is essentially a straight line between event and emotion. This is the reality that sometimes difficult things happen in life, and there will be a corresponding uncomfortable emotion attached to those events. This is normal, and healthy, and expected. We don't want to stop this connection of an event and the directly linked emotion, even when it is uncomfortable, because our emotional brains do need to process this stuff. We don't want to get into the habit of suppressing and ignoring our emotions and bottling them up, and then exploding or breaking down later on—which is far more uncomfortable in the long run!

Here's an example of what direct discomfort looks like:

EVENT	
A fight with a good friend	

EMOTIONS/THOUGHTS

Thought: I can't believe she said that to me.

Feelings: Sadness, Disappointment, Hurt, Betrayal, Anger

Based on the event, it makes total sense that you'd feel those emotions in relation to the fight. These are the feelings we want to sit with, allow, and learn to tolerate when they show up, even if it's hard, and even when it hurts.

What we *don't* want to do is get into the web of *indirect* discomfort. This is when the original event leads us off of this straight line and into a web of other partially related thoughts that aren't currently happening to us: memories, fears, and all of their associated emotions. This is when we can spiral and get overwhelmed. We want to help train our brains to allow the straight-line connection of emotional experiencing, but to avoid the temptation to stray into the web of associated brain memories that often get triggered and that lead us into a spiral of being emotionally overwhelmed. This takes a bit of compassionate discipline and gentle redirecting of the brain and the thoughts.

On the next page is an example of what indirect discomfort might look like.

EVENT

A fight with a friend

EMOTIONS / THOUGHTS

Sadness, Disappointment, Hurt, Betrayal, Anger

(This is ideally where we would halt our thinking process–beyond here is indirect discomfort)

Thought: Maybe none of my friends actually like me at all.

Thought: This is just like the time in grade 5 when Tommy got mad at me for missing his birthday party when I was sick.

Feelings: Rejection, Loneliness, Abandonment, Hopelessness

Thought: No one understands me. No one is there for me. I'm so alone.

Feelings: Despair, Withdrawal, Paralyzed, Distraught, Isolated

Thought: Everyone is just mad at me all the time. I'm never going to be happy if everyone hates me all the time.

Thought: Even my own parents must hate me. They get mad at me, too.

Thought: And Jenny was mad at me the other day, and Zack was upset a few days ago, and even my dog seems mad at me now.

Feelings: Overwhelmed, Frustrated, Confused, Attacked, Angry, Wanting to Lash Out

As you can see, one difficult event can quickly turn into a spiral of despair in our heads. This is what often makes us so hesitant to experience *any* difficult or unpleasant emotion, because we may not know how to stop the barrage of associated memories and thoughts from coming with it.

Everything we experience in our lives is associated with similar memories and patterns in our head. So when our brains think of something sad, we tend to think of a *whole bunch* of sad things, all at once. But we want to learn the skill of just sticking with one cause-and-effect association at a time. We aren't built to be able to process seventeen different challenging memories all at once. We have to help our brains stay focused, while at the same time noting any other thoughts that may come up as something we may want to revisit later—when we're not still processing the current event. We can always come back to old stuff again at a different time. But let's not do it all at once!

let's try it

Think of a current or recent difficult event, and the associated thoughts and feelings you had directly related to that event, then write these down in the boxes below. This is the direct discomfort that we want to allow ourselves to feel, process, and tolerate.

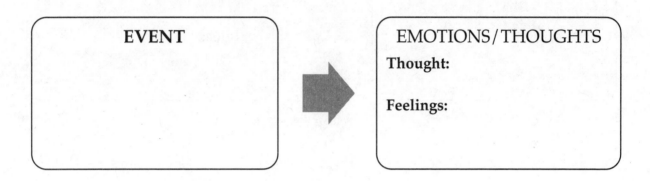

Now, let's look at what your web of indirect discomfort might have been, related to that event. Start with the same two boxes again below, and draw out any associated thoughts, feelings, emotions, and memories that may have come up when you thought about that original memory. Circle or highlight anything that might be a direct thought or emotion, and then put a star next to everything else as a note that you want to come back to and process or think about those things at a later time, when your brain isn't busy processing this current emotion. Just notice the web, and help your brain stay focused on the direct discomfort. Use your distress-tolerance skills for the difficult emotions that show up, reminding yourself that this isn't the moment to try to process your whole life, and every difficult situation you've ever had, all at once.

```
┌─────────────────────────┐      ┌─────────────────────────┐
│                         │      │  EMOTIONS / THOUGHTS    │
│         EVENT           │  ⇨   │  Thought:               │
│                         │      │                         │
│                         │      │  Feelings:              │
│                         │      │                         │
└─────────────────────────┘      └─────────────────────────┘
```

Now that you can see how your web works, what are some things you can say to yourself to help your brain stay focused on the straight line, direct discomfort, when it starts to derail into the web of indirect discomfort?

_____

_____

_____

_____

_____

_____

more to try

Each indirect upsetting memory that came up in the last exercise also deserves time and attention, but you can't do it all at once. Let's map out a plan for how you can stay focused on direct discomfort while avoiding the spiral trap of indirect discomfort.

Who can you go to for support or to talk to about any of these thoughts or memories? (For example, friends, loved ones, teachers, mentors.)

_____

_____

_____

What ways do you process difficult thoughts and feelings best? (For example, thinking and feeling while journaling, talking it out with someone, talking to yourself, going for a run or a walk, drawing or painting, or playing an instrument.)

_____

_____

_____

_____

Over the next few weeks, can you write down a few times when you can focus on processing some of the memories of the indirect discomfort web that came up? (For example, after school, Sunday evenings, lunch breaks, workout times at the gym.)

_____

_____

_____

Write down your commitment to yourself to make time to revisit and process old hurts, memories, or challenges in your life. What times are you willing and able to dedicate?

_____

_____

If you get stuck, get overwhelmed, or don't know what to do next to process parts of your web of indirect discomfort, are you willing or able to seek support from a trusted person, a loved one, or from a professional (help lines, online help chats, school counselor, or private counseling)?

_____

Goal 3

Finding Your Strength

8 fear—turn "what if" into "I can"

When difficult times in life come up, they can often bring feelings of anxiety, uncertainty, or fear. Sometimes, when we think of new situations or challenging times ahead, we can get stuck in a bit of a paralyzed feeling of not knowing what to do, or feeling helpless or unsure. These feelings can make us feel like we would just rather… not. Or that we would rather do whatever we can to avoid a challenging situation like that in the first place. We come up with all sorts of fun ways to think ourselves out of those feelings. But there is a better way!

Let's take a quick look at the anxiety equation from CBT. This is a little mathy way of thinking about the things that cause anxiety.

$$anxiety = \frac{\uparrow danger}{\downarrow coping}$$

If you remember your fractions, this means that when our sense of how dangerous a situation is going to be (the top of the fraction) increases, it creates a higher value for anxiety on the other side of the fraction.

This also means that when our sense of being able to cope with a situation (the bottom of the fraction) feels really low, that *also* makes the value of anxiety much higher.

So we want to tackle the two parts of the fraction. We want to keep the reality of danger from escalating to unrealistic levels, but we also want to build up our ability to *cope with* difficult or challenging situations (which includes where and from whom we can seek help if we get stuck).

One of the ways to help you build up your ability to cope with difficult situations is to "follow the fear." This means you literally chase after those imagined worst-case scenarios, and keep confronting them as they jump around to all the worst possible outcomes. This helps your brain realize that even when bad things happen in life, you *do* have options and solutions, and support to get through tough times. This approach looks like this:

What if...*you go to try out for the sports team at school and you don't make it?*

You could...*try out for a local house league team instead and make new friends there.*

What if...*you don't make that team either?*

You could...*try a different sport, or think about taking private lessons in that sport.*

What if...*everyone laughs at you or makes fun of you because of how bad you are at it?*

You could...*laugh along with them and then say, "Yeah, I may not be the best at it, but it's still fun to try! I think it's more fun than going to the gym, and I'm also getting to learn something new!"*

Whatever the fear is, follow it, chase it down, then answer it. If you don't know the answer or aren't sure what you might do, write down who you can go to for help, ideas, or support!

let's try it

Try this approach on your own with a fear that you maybe have been holding on to in your life about trying something new:

What if… _____(insert your fear here)?

Now let's follow up with what you could do if that really did happen!

You could… _____

_____

Sometimes a new fear will pop up in this process. (Not always, so if there isn't a new fear…don't search for one! But if another fear pops up, write it down next below.)

What if… _____

Now go ahead and answer that one, too!

You could… _____

_____

Keep following it along, and remember, if you get stuck, write down who or where you can go for help if you aren't sure what to do next!

What if… _____

You could… _____

_____

What if… _____

You could… _____

_____

Use this approach for any other fears in your life that may come up as well!

more to try

Let's not forget about the top half of that equation:

$$anxiety = \frac{\uparrow danger}{\downarrow coping}$$

Let's have a quick look at some of the "thought traps" (also known as cognitive distortions in CBT) that might show up in our brain as a signal that danger has gone way, way up and out of proportion to reality:

- **All-or-Nothing Thinking:** I'm Perfect or I'm a Failure. This is when the brain has decided that if something isn't perfect, it's literally just the worst. But things aren't always so black and white—don't let the perfect be the enemy of the good. Would you rather it be perfect, or would you rather it be done? Because usually both can't happen together.

- **Overgeneralization:** If One Thing Sucks, Everything Sucks Forever. This is when our brain decides that some small negative is going to be that way forever, and only get worse, and that it will apply to everything else in our lives, too.

- **Disqualifying the Positive:** That Didn't Count Anyway. This is when we find reasons that good things in our lives "don't count" or we explain away positives instead of noticing them and celebrating them. However small they may be, they are still good things!

- **Jumping to Conclusions:** Of Course I'm Right (Mind-Reading and Fortune-Telling Error). Fortune telling is when we predict the future as if something is set in stone. But even if we think we have a good guess, we still can't know how things will turn out for sure, and those guesses shouldn't stop us from trying. Mind reading is when we decide for sure what someone thinks about us without them verifying or telling us. Sometimes we're not as good at guessing as we think we are, and we need to find out for sure before relying on these guesses as facts!

- **Catastrophizing:** It's the End of the World! This is when our brain jumps from one terrible thing to the next. For example, we fail a test and then imagine failing the course, then never graduating, then never having any money, then living on the streets homeless…that escalated quickly!

- **Emotional Reasoning:** I'm Sad, So Life Sucks. When our brains are in a sad mood, we often see many things through that sad lens—but when we are happy again a few hours later, suddenly things don't look so gloomy anymore. Try to watch out that your perspective of your life doesn't completely turn on its head when you have a bad day or bad week—it's just a temporary lens!

- **"Should" Statements:** Guilting Yourself While Not Changing Anything. When we tell ourselves we "should" do something, we just guilt ourselves while not changing anything. This can impact our mood significantly and actually make us less productive. Change "should" to "I will" or "I can" or "I plan to" or, for a fun twist, "I get to." Turn it into action or a plan, even if that plan isn't right now!

Write down here which thought traps you use most when your brain starts overestimating the danger of a situation or the impact of how bad something might be, feel, or turn out.

_____

_____

_____

_____

Write down here a way to help remind yourself to watch out for these thought traps (something to tell yourself, an alarm or reminder for yourself somewhere, something to put in your journal or agenda).

_____

_____

_____

Remember that your brain will always focus on the "tiny grain of truth"—the fact that there is always a possibility of the absolute worst-case scenario. But it usually isn't very likely, so we want to rebalance how definite that feeling or fear is. Once it is rebalanced by calling out the thought traps that are showing up, *then* go forth with that tiny grain of truth and start your "follow the fear" approach. Help your brain to realize that, even in the worst-case scenario, you *can* make it through. And if you don't know how to—there's always help. Always.

9 letter to yourself

let's get started

When life gets hard and throws you tough obstacles, it can feel much different in the moment than you expected. This may come as a surprise, which may make us further doubt our ability to handle whatever comes our way.

Let's talk a little bit about what goes on here. What happens in the brain is that we have cells called neurons that form connections and help us remember, learn, and store information. You can picture these almost as complex spider webs inside your brain—each spider web holds connected information. For instance, if you think of the concept of a birthday party, you're going to probably also think of a birthday cake, streamers, presents, and balloons. This is your "birthday party" spider web—your neural network of connected, similar information. This is also called a "schema."

When we are feeling good, confident, supported, and healthy, and we think about an upcoming difficult time, we will be thinking about tackling that time in our life while working from one of our happy, confident neural networks, or spider webs. On the other hand, when we are sad, frustrated, or feeling hopeless or defeated, we are going to have all of *those* spider webs activated, and the sad spider webs often don't connect over to the happy spider webs. In those moments, it can be very hard to get our brains to let go of the sad spider webs they have gotten stuck in.

let's try it

One of the best exercises to help your brain remember its confident spider webs when you're facing a tough situation is to write a letter to yourself—a letter from the happy, confident version of you, to the version of yourself that you know comes out when you're struggling most. You can read it back to yourself in some of your hardest moments, to help you access the happy spider webs when you get stuck.

For example, let's look at Anika's letter to herself:

Hey, Anika. It's that time again, isn't it? When life has turned upside down and you're feeling lost? Don't worry—we've been here before. It's rough, I know. I remember how it feels, to be stuck in that feeling of not knowing what to do next. I want to remind you that you have gotten through times like this before—even at the moments when you weren't sure you could handle all these feelings and emotions. And that life does get good again. I promise! Even if, right now, it seems like there's just no chance of that—remember that you're stuck in the negative spider webs right now. You have the positive thoughts sitting in your brain, too—they're just a bit hard to access right now. That's okay! We'll get through it.

Remember your friends. The people who love you and will be there for you—if you remember to ask them for help. Even if your brain right now is saying that no one cares or no one will be there for you, remember to give people a chance to be there for you, and to ask them for what you need. They have been there before, and they will show up again. Remember that they will be imperfect and may not get it completely right, but they are good people and they love you.

Deep breaths if you get frustrated—it's okay to feel frustrated. Give yourself some room to also be imperfect. Don't forget the simple things—to eat, sleep, and get outside for a walk.

Take care of yourself. Remember your strength. Remember that even when you thought you'd never smile or laugh again in tough times, that you have smiled, laughed, loved, and enjoyed so many things. I am here for you, and we will get through this thing together. You can do this. Just breathe. Slow down. And breathe again.

Take a separate piece of paper and try writing your own version—something that works for you. Consider taking a picture of it and keeping it on your phone, so you can access it any time. Or type it up and store it in your email or notes on your phone, or somewhere else that you can always find it.

If you find yourself getting stuck or not knowing what to say, think of what a loving friend, family member, or mentor might say to you who you've found helpful in the past. Or try Googling some ideas of positive or motivational things you can say to yourself. Some people also like to take a video of themselves speaking this to themselves, so they can watch it when they need to.

more to try

You can also select a few mantras to inspire yourself. These can be a few words, or a sentence or two. They can be song lyrics, quotes, or even just words or phrases that you make up yourself. I've seen people put them on jewelry, on T-shirts, or on other items they keep close to them to help them through tough times.

Some examples I often hear from people are similar to these ones below:

"This too shall pass."

"You can do this, you're stronger than you know."

"Keep breathing, keep moving, one foot in front of the other."

"It's uncomfortable, but you can handle it. It hurts, but it won't kill you."

"Pain is temporary, and your strength knows no bounds. This will make you stronger."

Write your mantra to encourage yourself below. You can make it fancy, in calligraphy, in color, or just simple and straightforward. Whatever works for you. Consider also writing it down in your phone or taking a picture of it for yourself, or keeping it on a piece of paper in your wallet or purse, so it can always be nearby. Or you can include it in your letter to yourself.

_____

_____

_____

_____

10 vulnerability: finding the strength to be yourself

let's get started

There's a lot of pressure in our society today to be the "perfect" version of ourselves—online, on social media, and even in public or around our friends. So the idea of failure... well, that can feel pretty intimidating. People might judge us, or look down on us, or laugh at us. That can seem really hard to get through and can leave us playing it safe in life, instead of following our dreams.

If we have been playing it safe, it's often even scarier to fully engage in the messiness of life, because that requires us to be vulnerable. Vulnerability means to be seen and, often, to be judged. The important thing to remember is that judgment from other people really has a whole lot less to do with *you* than it has to do with *them*. There's a wonderful quote that one of my favorite authors, Brené Brown, uses a lot—the quote originally comes from Theodore Roosevelt, and is an excerpt from his speech "Citizenship in a Republic," which he delivered in 1910:

It is not the critic who counts; not the man who points out how the strong man stumbles, or where the doer of deeds could have done them better. The credit belongs to the man who is actually in the arena, whose face is marred by dust and sweat and blood; who strives valiantly; who errs, who comes short again and again, because there is no effort without error and shortcoming; but who does actually strive to do the deeds; who knows great enthusiasms, the great devotions; who spends himself in a worthy cause; who at the best knows in the end the triumph of high achievement, and who at the worst, if he fails, at least fails while daring greatly, so that his place shall never be with those cold and timid souls who neither know victory nor defeat.

So yes, people may judge, and they may laugh, but remember that their response is often just a defense mechanism, the sort of thing we all sometimes fall into when we are reminded of our own fears and our own vulnerabilities.

Inside of *you*, you have that strength and ability to try, to stumble, to fall, and to fail—and to still get through it and try again. But it starts with learning to get comfortable with vulnerability—which can be one of the hardest things in life. So let's start getting comfortable with our own vulnerability now.

let's try it

We all have parts of ourselves that we tend to show to the world quite easily. Our strengths, the things we are good at, or the things we are proud of. But we all also have things that we aren't as sure about, or that we aren't as comfortable with. We often don't want people to know these things about us, because they make us feel vulnerable. If people criticize these parts of us, it can feel extra painful, because they are our tender spots. But remember: *People can only use against you that which you haven't yet faced yourself.*

So let's get to know both sides of ourselves—our "outer" self that we show the world, and the parts of our "inner" self that we may guard more carefully.

The Side of Yourself that You Show the World (the Public You): This first mask on the next page represents the side you usually show the world. Write some words below the mask on the next page about what this "public facing" version of yourself is like. What do you usually show the world about yourself, and how does this feel? If you wish, you can also modify the mask, either by drawing in some additional parts (adding colors, images, or words) or by pasting over it with a face that you found online or cut out from a magazine. It may even be a picture of your own face from a certain time that you relate to the "Public You." (You can also draw a larger mask on a separate sheet of paper if you want more space to do this exercise and get even more creative!)

_____

_____

_____

_____

_____

_____

The Side of Yourself that Usually Stays Hidden (the Inner You): This second mask represents the side you usually do *not* show the world—what's behind or on the back of your "public" mask. Write some words about what this "Inner You" version of yourself is like. What do you usually keep more private about yourself, and why, and how does this feel? Again, if you wish, you can modify this mask, either by drawing some additional parts or by pasting over it with a face that you found online or cut out from a magazine.

_____

_____

_____

_____

_____

_____

more to try

Looking at these two "sides" of yourself, what did you learn about yourself while doing this exercise?

_____

_____

_____

Imagine that the second mask was on the flip side of the first mask, back-to-back, so you could change masks just by turning them around. What do you think would happen if you turned your usual "outer self" mask around and lived that way for a day—so that the world saw your "inner" self instead of the "outer" self that you usually present?

_____

_____

_____

What would be the worst that could happen if you spent a day with your mask reversed?

_____

_____

How could you handle it if this _did_ actually happen? What could you do to get through it?

_____

_____

_____

What would be the best thing that could happen if you turned this mask around?

_____

_____

What would happen if no one ever saw the back of your mask until the day you died?

_____

_____

What would you gain by never showing anyone the back of your mask?

_____

_____

_____

What would you lose by never showing anyone the back of your mask?

_____

_____

_____

How would you *like* to be able to live your life? Do you have a desire to be able to be your true self, at all times, and be accepted for that person? If yes, what do you think it would take to be able to do that?

_____

_____

_____

_____

_____

11 taking chances

let's get started

Oftentimes in life, when we feel vulnerable or we have to take chances and risk failure, we may try to numb out or block out the negative emotions or outcomes in life. The problem is, when we try to block out negative emotions, we also block out positive ones. Let's look at the following example:

Scenario 1: Kyle really liked one of his fellow classmates, Shonda. They had been friends for awhile, but he was starting to realize that he liked her as more than just a friend. He thought about asking her out, but the thought of her saying no, of her not being interested in return, felt too scary. To avoid feeling hurt by her rejection, he never told her how he felt about her and he never asked her out. Shonda ended up assuming that he only liked her as a friend, and so she pursued another relationship with Sanjay. Kyle looked on as the girl he liked dated another guy.

Scenario 2: Kyle realized he wanted to date Shonda, and he really didn't know how it would turn out. He was scared of her saying no and rejecting him—and feared she might even laugh at him. That would be awful! But then he realized that if she did laugh at him, well, then she wasn't the kind of girl he wanted to date anyway, so it would be okay if she said no. He also realized that if he asked her out and she said no, at least he would know that he tried, and wouldn't live in a state of regret if she did end up dating someone else instead. He also realized that this would be the only way she might ever say yes! If he never tried, then he would never know. He realized it was going to be worth the risk to give it a try, even though it was going to feel pretty scary and intimidating—it was going to be worth it, no matter the outcome.

let's try it

I want you to think of something that's really important to you (friendship, relationship, career, achievement, sports, a dream, or a goal you have). Maybe it's getting into a certain school. Maybe it's having a certain something as part of your life. Think of that thing that you really want or are really passionate about, but that you are also feeling kind of scared might not work out. Now, take a separate piece of paper and write down your biggest fear about this topic. (For example: "I will end up alone, forever—no one will ever love me.")

Okay. Now turn the piece of paper over, and on the other side write the exact opposite of that fear. (For example: "I will be happy and in love. I will have someone in my life who accepts me and loves me for who I really am.")

Okay. Now, flip back briefly and look at what you wrote on the other side of the page. Your biggest fear. Ugh. Scary to look at, right?

Now what if I told you that, today, for a once-in-a-lifetime chance, I have added a magic pixie dust to that piece of paper, so that if you tore it up and threw it away it would take that fear away from you forever? So you'd never have to deal with that fear ever again. Poof! It would be gone from your life. What an opportunity! Tempting…right? Gosh, to think about living without that fear hanging over your head—what a relief!

But wait! The magic pixie dust makes anything else on that paper disappear. It will take your fear away—but what's on the opposite side of the page from your fear?

Oh, right. Your dream.

You would have to give that up, too.

If you choose to throw away that paper in order to give up that fear, you also have to give up that dream. You have to give it away as well, and you can never have it again.

Are you still willing to throw away that paper and give away both your fear *and your dream*?

☐ Yes   ☐ No

I have asked hundreds of people this question, and so far no one has actually been willing to take me up on this offer—maybe at first they think they will, but if they sit with the reality of giving up their dream for a little while, everyone so far has ended up holding on to their piece of paper. Because, when it comes down to it, a little fear (or even a *lot* of fear) is a small price to pay for the opportunity to maybe get what you are really after in life. To know that you tried—that you gave it a shot, even if it didn't work out. And that if it didn't work out, to be willing to keep trying, because you know it's important to you.

As Jim Carrey once put it, "You can fail at what you don't want, so you might as well take a chance on doing what you love."

more to try

The second half of this exercise is about overcoming that rejection or that failure, especially after you have put yourself out there and making yourself vulnerable. So let's give it a little bit of thought.

We all have our battles, our disappointments, our failures, and our rejections. Even the people you might assume to be free of these hardships have experienced these things—trust me, it's true. So here, I want you to think of some of your idols or role models. Pick a few of the people you admire, and look up their deeper stories. Some good ones to start with might be Oprah, Keanu Reeves, J. K. Rowling, Dwayne Johnson, Bethany Hamilton, Jim Carrey, Jennifer Hudson, Nick Vujicic, Nicki Minaj, Stephen King, and Charlize Theron. All these people have inspiring stories about overcoming adversity, as have many other people, whether they're famous or not. Pick out some of them you can relate to, and keep their stories in mind whenever you are facing your own adversities. Make some notes below about what you find, and add your reflections.

_____

_____

_____

_____

Next ask a mentor, loved one, or someone you admire about a time they were rejected and initially upset, but then later realized that it worked out for the best in the end. Write their story below, and add any of your reflections. Ask them what they learned from this experience, or how it added to or changed their life as it is now.

_____

_____

_____

_____

What did you learn from these stories about rejection, hardship, failure, and hard times in life? What do you want to tell yourself for times you are rejected, or initially fail at something, or have a hard time with something in your life? Write this message to yourself below.

_____

_____

_____

_____

_____

_____

_____

_____

assertive defense of the self

let's get started

One of the other big things that can keep us feeling stuck is the fear of how others might respond to us, or what they might say to us that could be scary or hurtful. We may play this out in our heads—imagining people getting mad at us, making fun of us, or challenging us at times when we feel most vulnerable. The fear of what others might say to us can keep us from trying new things or being open to failing or to screwing up or to getting messy as we are learning and growing in life. But there is something we can do about it!

To do this exercise, all you need to do is start with what you are worried people might say or think about you (Padesky, 1997). Once you have that feared thought, you then just imagine what you could actually say in response—even if you never actually say it out loud in real life. But if you imagine yourself saying it inside your own head, at least it's right there, ready to go, if you do ever need it in real life.

This is known as "assertive" defense of the self—not "aggressive" (attacking back at the other person). This is an important distinction. While you do this exercise, remember that the goal is to focus on your own strength and your own worth, in order to gently but assertively deflect any rude, mean, unhelpful, or unnecessary comments or judgments from other people. This isn't free rein to attack another person—because then we would just be part of the cycle that we are trying to get away from.

Let's look at an example. Imagine that you are Erin, and that Riley is the person you are worried about being negative toward you, and that you just gave a presentation in class.

Riley: Wow, Erin, that was really terrible. Like, super embarrassing, actually. You're so awkward. Didn't you practice at all?

Erin (You): I'm sorry you feel that way, Riley, but I did the best I could. Presentations are something I am working on to get better at. Everyone has to start somewhere, and I'm proud of the work I did and how far I've come. It may not have been perfect, but I'm really happy that I gave it my best shot and took a chance.

Riley: Don't be such a baby. I was just making a comment. If you were tough, you'd be able to take a little bit of criticism, and not just cry about it. Jeez.

Erin (You): Thank you for your concern, Riley. However, I know I did my best and I'd prefer to just leave it at that.

Do you see the pattern here? We are actually focusing very little on Riley and the comments that Riley is making—and continuing to focus on ourselves. By not engaging Riley, and instead focusing on our own strengths, intentions, and goals, we don't escalate Riley or further the conversation (which, by the looks of it, wouldn't have been productive anyway). We are staying out of the conflict, while at the same time reinforcing and asserting our own strengths, intentions, and goals.

let's try it

Try your assertive defense below! Think of something you are worried about trying, that you might mess up the first time you try it. Remember, failing or messing up is basically a part of learning anything. We even had to fail (and fall!) when we were learning to walk. Imagine if you gave up trying to walk after a few tries—you'd never be where you are in life, now. (Literally!) Every new thing, and everything we want to get better at, will require us to be imperfect—it's actually a good sign! It means we're learning and growing.

What are you worried people will say if you fail or mess up at something new you are trying to get better at?

_____

_____

What can you say in response to assertively defend yourself? (Hint: focus on yourself, not the other person.)

_____

_____

Carry on the script from here—write out exactly what you are worried about, and what you could say back to another person. If you get stuck somewhere, not knowing what to say, try asking a wise loved one, mentor, or friend what they might say, and see if that helps you get any ideas. Or, imagine it was a friend in the situation instead of yourself— what might a friend say to assertively defend themselves if confronted by someone?

_____

_____

_____

_____

more to try

The next important thing to know when looking at assertive defense of the self is that it can really seem like the comments are all about us. I mean, the person is usually addressing us directly and talking about us specifically, so that means it's completely about us…right?

That's a trick question, of course. There's often a lot of other stuff going on in these interactions that doesn't have much to do with us. For instance, our parents might be hard on us or judgmental because they are actually worried about their own critics in their own lives, and want to protect both you and themselves from someone else who's going to judge or make comments if things don't appear "perfect." Or maybe a friend is harsh on you because she is worried that the way you look or appear is going to impact her. Maybe some teachers are really critical of you because you remind them of themselves a little too much, and they end up subconsciously projecting on you. Really, most of the time when people are hard on us, it has a lot less to do with us and a whole lot more to do with them.

Read this story to help you with a metaphor to understand what people may be carrying.

You are in a beautiful oasis in the middle of the desert, sipping your favorite drink. You are looking out over the desert, enjoying the view and the weather, when across the sand dunes you notice a man in the distance. He seems to be carrying a large box in his arms, and he's heading in your direction. You watch as he struggles and stumbles his way through the deep sand. You are captivated—you want to hear his story. So you finish your drink and go to meet him.

You greet him at the edge of the oasis and offer to take the box he has been carrying. He is very relieved to be freed of the weight, and thanks you profusely as you lead him over to the watering hole and help to fetch him a drink. You sit at a table together and you listen to his story with rapt attention—the story of his trials and tribulations that have brought him this far. The box sits on the table between you. He continues to share his story, and after a few more drinks it has become time for him to be on his way. He thanks you from the bottom of his heart, telling you how much this has meant to him. You both stand up to part ways, pushing your chairs back—and you are left with a decision.

The box is still sitting on the table.

As you see him look over at the box, cringing with the idea of him picking it back up after having only just regained his strength, part of you wants to step in and offer to take it for him. It will be so difficult to see him pick up that heavy weight again. Your heart hurts just to think about it.

If you follow this part of your heart—if you take the box and this man leaves without it—it turns out that the box is magical. It simply duplicates itself—it is now in your arms, as well as manifesting again in the arms of the man who just left. You now both have a copy of this box. You struggle to figure out what to do with it—but as you scramble to open the box, you learn that it is closed to you. It will not open to you and show you its contents. So what do you do now?

Let's go back to the moment of decision again and see if there is another way this could have played out.

As you and the man stand up to part ways, while part of your heart hurts to see him pick the box back up, another part of you realizes that this box must be truly important to him. You realize that, at any moment on his journey across the desert, he could have chosen to put the box down and leave it behind. You realize that, in some way, he needed to carry this box—you might not know all the reasons why he is continuing to carry the box, but you know that it is his decision to keep it, as well as when to open it and work through the contents to make the load lighter, or to find a way to put the box down altogether.

If you take the box from him, you would actually be doing him a disservice. You can share your space with him, you can listen to him talk about the box, and you can help him carry the weight for a time, but when you part ways, the box is his to take with him. You cannot keep it for him, and you cannot do the work for him either.

I hope you can see that the "box" in question here is a metaphor for the challenges or unresolved issues that each person might be carrying. We can't take on other people's issues or challenges. We can't take their box from them—it's not ours to take. They are the only ones who can do this work. Sometimes people may ask us to take their boxes—or even *throw* the boxes at us that they wish they didn't have—but we still can't do the work for them. We need to ask ourselves, "What is ours to own, and what is not ours to own?"

Questions:

What boxes might your family or friends be carrying?

_____

_____

_____

What boxes might you have picked up along the way that aren't actually yours to carry?

_____

_____

_____

What would happen if you put that box back down or gave it back to the original owner?

_____

_____

_____

What would be the worst thing that could happen if you put down a box that wasn't yours?

_____

_____

_____

What would be the best thing that could happen if you put down a box that wasn't yours?

_____

_____

_____

Why is it important to not carry baggage or boxes that aren't your own?

_____

_____

_____

How can you use this idea to help you face your fears of failure regarding how it applies to other people's responses around you?

_____

_____

_____

_____

There is resilience in having boundaries—knowing whose box is whose, and what is yours to own, and what is not yours to own. Remember this box metaphor for all these aspects of your life.

Goal 4

Keeping Perspective

13 self-care

let's get started

Of all the different components of resilience, self-care can be one of the hardest skills to learn. Self-care can be anything and everything that helps you take care of *you*. In life, there is usually an awful lot of pressure to go, go, go, and keep pushing on even when we are wearing thin. This can lead us to illness, injury, or low mental health days. Likewise, when we are hitting a hard time in life, sometimes we can feel pressure to appear "strong" and not let our emotions show—by pushing ourselves too hard or burning the candle at both ends to keep up appearances.

Well, this is where we are going to break apart those narratives that tell us we have to do those things—because they aren't true! It's healthy, normal, and *highly* recommended to have self-care in your life in all times. And when things get rough, to increase this self-care even further.

So what is self-care? It can get a bit tricky to know what is self-care, and what is merely distraction or avoidance.

If you have any social media accounts you follow on wellness or mental health, you may have read up on different popular ways to engage in "self-care." These include things like bubble baths, reading a book, listening to music, doing yoga, going to the gym, coloring, watching a movie, going for a walk in nature, or other things that you find enjoyable. These can all be great! But one thing that is not so often mentioned in traditional self-care advice is to notice how you feel *after* you have done one of those "self-care" activities. Do you feel better and have a bit more energy? Or do you feel more drained or more anxious after you do it, and find it equally if not more difficult to get back to the other tasks you have to do that day?

Self-care isn't always a matter of spoiling yourself or doing something fun or exciting or luxurious. Sometimes it is self-care to also make sure you engage in the basics of your life—eating, sleeping, basic hygiene and chores, and exercising well. It's saying yes to some activities, and sometimes saying no to others.

Every person is different. Let's try an exercise to help you find out which things are self-care specifically for *you*!

let's try it

When you're feeling stretched thin, or you're going through a hard time, or you are low on energy or resources, try a few of these items below. Then, after you've tried them, in the column next to the item, take note of whether you feel better, worse, or the same as you did before you did that activity. This way, you can learn which things actually help give you energy *back*—not just distract you temporarily without making you actually feel better in the long run.

Self-Care Activity	Did you feel better, worse, or the same after doing the self-care activity?	If it helped, what mood did this help you with?
Go for a walk		
Play with animals		
Get a hug from someone		
Write in a journal		
Read a book		
Play a game for a short while		
Meditate (use an app or YouTube for help)		
Do yoga or play a sport		

Self-Care Activity	Did you feel better, worse, or the same after doing the self-care activity?	If it helped, what mood did this help you with?
Cook or bake some food		
Take a shower or bath		
Take a nap		
Get a task done from your to-do list		
Make social plans with a friend		
Say no to something that can be optional if you're overwhelmed		
Ask for help from someone		
Use a chat service or phone line for support ("7 Cups of Tea," mental health helplines)		
Watch funny videos online		
Light a candle		
Organize or clean something		

Self-Care Activity	Did you feel better, worse, or the same after doing the self-care activity?	If it helped, what mood did this help you with?
Make a schedule		
Write a to-do list and prioritize		
Sing or play an instrument		
Punch a pillow or yell into a pillow to release energy		
Take a class in boxing or a martial art		
(Write a few of your own below!)		

You can also make some mental notes about how long you did each activity, or what time of the day each activity was most helpful, or if you did the activity alone or with someone else, or any other details that might be important to remember.

more to try: supportive relationships

The next step to add to your self-care plan is to make note of other people and other relationships that you can turn to if you're not doing well or are starting to run out of energy. There are lots of different types of people in our lives, and some people will be good at supporting us in certain ways, and other people in our lives will play other roles. Think of the people in your own life, and see if you can jot down a few of them to turn to for each of these kinds of things. Most often these will be people in your family, your friends, mentors, teachers, or even sometimes health professionals. Sometimes they might even be people whose videos you watch on YouTube—or it might even be yourself! Have a look below and write some ideas down for yourself. Then turn back to this page at times in your life when you need a little extra boost from someone in your support system. You can write down as many people for each question as you can think of, or it might just be one person, depending on the question and who is part of your life right now.

Who can you talk to who helps cheer you up? Someone who might be funny, who has a positive perspective, or who always has a good joke?

_____

_____

_____

Who can you turn to for advice? Who might be a person who can help give you wise direction and solid advice without judging you or forcing you to take a certain path at the same time?

_____

_____

_____

Who can you turn to for space to feel your feelings? Someone you can talk to who lets you be sad if you are sad, and lets you be angry if you are angry—who can be comfortable with emotions?

_____

_____

_____

Who can you talk to about personal issues or concerns? Someone who is trustworthy and who won't share your secrets or tell other people about your conversations if you need them to be private right now?

_____

_____

_____

Who can you turn to for inspiration? People who help you see things in a different way, or who inspire you through their words or actions, or even just the way they may live their life?

_____

_____

_____

Who can you hang around with or talk to if you need some energy? Someone who lights you up and raises you up and motivates you to get active and engage in more things?

_____

_____

_____

Who can you hang out with or talk to for fun, or for some lighthearted, feel-good times that lift your mood and make you feel generally good?

_____

_____

_____

Is there anyone else you can think of who you can turn to for other things you may need? List those people and your relationships with them below.

_____

_____

_____

Now, if you feel that there aren't as many people in your life to fill those roles as you'd like, and you wish you had a few more people in some of those categories, make some notes of ideas of where you might be able to meet more people and build more friendships or other healthy relationships. It might be volunteering, clubs or organisations at your school, friends of friends, or through a new job or travel experience that you can think of. It might be building on current friendships and seeing if you can help build them to a new level; or it may be looking into professional resources, like a counselor, or online resource, or community as well. Write down some of your thoughts below!

_____

_____

_____

_____

_____

_____

14 mindfulness

let's get started

There's a really interesting saying that we often use in counseling: "Depression lives in the past, anxiety lives in the future, and peace lives in the present." While this may be a slight oversimplification, it sheds light on some of the thought traps we often fall into that can impact our mood in difficult ways. When we dwell on the past and think too much about things we can't change, that can impact our mood. When we worry about the future and things we can't control, that also impacts our mood. Too often, we forget to live wholly in the present. In fact, living in the present can be quite a difficult skill to learn. Animals and young children are usually really great at this skill, but somewhere along the way, we often find it more and more difficult as we get older.

Enter the mindfulness movement.

To be mindful is to focus 100% (or as much as you can) on what you are doing at that exact moment. It's a bit different from meditation, which often asks you to be seated or still and focused on your breathing and your thoughts. Mindfulness aims to connect you to *whatever* it is you are doing in the moment, and to focus on that—not the past, not the future.

To do this best, we use our five senses. This is because our five senses are always in the present moment—they can ground us and connect us to exactly what we are doing, and can get us out of our heads.

Mindfulness is a great way to help yourself focus under pressure, because if you are doing something difficult, and while doing it you're busy just imagining all the hundreds of ways it can go wrong or what people are going to think of you, you'll likely lose focus and not perform as well. If you can stay in the moment, you can often stay much more focused—even under pressure.

let's try it

Here are a few ways to practice doing different activities mindfully.

1. *Breathing*: If you are sitting still, going for a drive, or just generally feeling a little overwhelmed, you can mindfully breathe anywhere you go. Notice your five senses, and try breathing in the "square" pattern—breathe in for four seconds, hold your breath for four seconds, breathe out for four seconds, and hold your breath for four seconds. Or just make sure your exhale is longer than your inhale. For instance, count three seconds inhale, and five seconds exhale to start, and see if you can extend it longer.

   a. **Touch:** Notice your lungs expanding and collapsing as you breathe. Notice the feeling of the air through your nose and mouth. Notice temperature and body sensations and your heartbeat. Notice the tension in your body, and work to relax it as you breathe.

   b. **Sight:** Focus on one focal point at a time in front of you and note the size, texture, shapes, shadows, colors, and more as you breathe in and out.

   c. **Sound:** Focus on the sounds of the air moving in and out of your lungs.

   d. **Smell:** Focus on the smells, or light a scented candle to help focus your mind.

2. *Walking*: Go for a walk—outside if the weather permits, but otherwise in the building you are in (maybe just down a hallway and back). If possible, a walk in nature is the best for this exercise!

   a. **Touch:** What do your feet feel like as they hit the floor? Notice the shift in weight in your body, the muscles tensing and relaxing, and the way your body moves as you walk. Notice your breath, and focus on breathing in and out.

b. **Sight:** What do you see as you are walking? Notice the details—the shadows, textures, shades, and shapes. What details do you maybe normally miss if this is somewhere you walk often? If this is a new place you are walking, notice the details and make note of the interesting things around you as you go.

c. **Sound:** What do your feet sound like as they hit the floor or the ground? What other sounds are around you? Stop and take note of the sounds, and then walk forward again and notice if things sound different as you are walking versus standing still.

d. **Smell:** Breathe in the air around you deeply. If it is fresh outdoor air, notice how that air smells different than inside your home or in other buildings.

e. **Taste (optional for this exercise):** Notice this if it applies on your walk. Are you carrying a cup of coffee? Or a bottle of cold water? Notice the taste and texture if you are also eating or drinking. Notice the taste of fresh air as you breathe in if you are outside.

You can do just about anything during your day mindfully. Slow your mind down and try to focus on the present moment, taking your brain out from future or past thoughts, worries, or even to-do items. The more you practice this, the easier it gets. And the more you practice, the easier it will be to do under pressure when times get tough. Work to extend your focus and to gently redirect your thoughts if you find your mind wanders, but do this without judgment.

more to try: emotion regulation

Part of why mindfulness helps you stay focused under pressure is because it regulates your emotions. In therapy, we use the term "emotion regulation" to mean the ability to halt an escalating anxiety spike, or to stop a low-mood spiral from continuing downward, or to calm a rising anger outburst before you explode or say something you might regret later.

When we get caught in our thoughts, or if we are spiraling in our mood and emotions, we can apply some mindfulness to help get out of our heads and into our bodies instead.

Below, write down a few moments when you found yourself getting upset, anxious, or angry, but were able to keep yourself from escalating and acting or reacting in ways you know you didn't want to. What are your success strategies for calming yourself and regulating your emotions?

A time I was getting very upset, sad, angry, etc…	What I did to help calm myself and stay focused…

With each of the examples, consider these questions as well:

1. What might have happened or gone differently if I *hadn't* moderated my mood?

2. What reactions do I most commonly have that I want to continue to work to manage and reduce (for example, getting angry, withdrawing, or giving up), using these calming strategies when I can?

3. What other strategies have I learned through this book so far (mindfulness, etc.) that might help me even more in the future that I can try during tough moments like these?

Once you have a few good ideas of how you manage those difficult emotions best, think about cultivating and improving those strategies, and focus on practicing doing them mindfully—in the present moment—even during times when you aren't so upset (such as calm breathing, etc.).

The more you learn to flex those muscles and practice those strategies, the easier they will be to access, and the more helpful they will be to you during times you are most upset in your life.

values chart— 15
what drives you?

Going through stressful life situations is hard! It can take a lot of energy and a lot of positive self-talk to get through it, and—let's be honest—it can be pretty uncomfortable, frustrating, or even discouraging at times.

One of the best ways to help stay on track with your goals and push through even the hardest times is to get in touch with what's most important to you. Let's look at an example.

Cho wanted to become a police officer. She knew it was going to be incredibly hard to get a position on the force, both physically and mentally. She knew there was a physical fitness test as part of the testing process before one was even considered for an interview. She practiced the running, lifting, climbing, and everything else she had to do over and over again, but when she went to do her test, things just didn't come together that day. She didn't meet the minimum requirements. She was devastated.

It would have been really easy to give up at this point, and just move on to something else. Why bother? Maybe it just wasn't meant to be.

But then Cho remembered why this was so important to her. She knew that she had a very strong sense of justice, accountability, community, and leadership. She remembered that, despite how hard this was going to be, it was going to be worth it for her. So she was going to train even harder and push herself even further, because this was a really important job that she had always felt super passionate about. As Cho remembered her values and thought about the big picture for her life, she was able to push past those initial feelings of discomfort. She continued training, with the help of a professional trainer this time, and the next time she did her test, she passed!

let's get started

The following list can help you get a sense of what values are most important to you. You'll probably agree to a certain degree with most things on this list, so I want you to try to not think too hard here about your answers. I want you to *feel* as you read each word—which one resonates with you on that deeper, gut level? Which words make you go, "Yeah, *that* one!" Circle the words that make you feel that feeling the most. People tend to pick somewhere between five and fifteen words to start this exercise, to help you as a guide. If you think of a word that isn't here, you can add it yourself.

accountability	altruism	service	vulnerability
diversity	efficiency	belonging	speed
humility	inquisitiveness	enthusiasm	challenge
security	self-reliance	intuition	expertise
accuracy	ambition	boldness	legacy
independence	elegance	equality	spontaneity
self-actualization	insightfulness	joy	love
achievement	sensitivity	simplicity	stability
financial security	assertiveness	relationships	security
ingenuity	empathy	calmness	commitment
self-control	intelligence	excellence	expressiveness
adventurousness	serenity	authenticity	loyalty
effectiveness	balance	justice	strategy
inner harmony	enjoyment	carefulness	community
selflessness	intellectual status	leadership	fairness

making a difference	freedom	curiosity	diligence
strength	originality	growth	holiness
compassion	thankfulness	nature	reliability
faith	cooperation	practicality	honesty
mastery	fun	traditionalism	discretion
perseverance	patriotism	environmentalism	honor
structure	thoroughness	decisiveness	restraint
competitiveness	correctness	happiness	vitality
merit	generosity	preparedness	aesthetics
success	perfection	trustworthiness	playfulness
consistency	thoughtfulness	dependability	propriety
fitness	courtesy	hard work	humor
obedience	goodness	professionalism	education
support	helpfulness	truth-seeking	courage
contentment	piety	determination	respect
openness	timeliness	health	communication
teamwork	creativity	prudence	passion
contribution	grace	understanding	flexibility
focus	positivity	devoutness	recognition
order	accuracy	personal growth	discipline
temperance	beauty	helping society	invention
control	tolerance	uniqueness	responsibility

duty	purpose	gratitude	imagination
kindness	bravery	logic	wisdom
knowledge	ethics	precision	credibility
experiences	modesty	unity	_____
entertainment	expression	productivity	_____
sacrifice	solitude	craftsmanship	_____
safety	family	profitability	_____
empowerment	fashion	hospitality	_____
meaning	collaboration	wealth	_____

Once you have your top words circled, focus in on those. Try to pick out your top five—the words that resonated most deeply within you as you read them and thought about them. Rank them below, with number 1 being your most important value.

1. _____

2. _____

3. _____

4. _____

5. _____

Think about how you currently have each of these values in your life right now. Write down areas in your life that are currently fulfilling or connecting with each of these values.

1. _____

2. _____

3. _____

4. _____

5. _____

Now think about areas of your life that you'd like to grow or develop in the future, and how they might connect to each of your top five values. This could be around certain experiences, achievements, relationships, situations, jobs, volunteering, personal goals, and more.

1. _____

2. _____

3. _____

4. _____

5. _____

Next time you are finding it a challenge to persevere in the face of stress, remember your values and what's driving you toward those goals in the first place.

more to do

Before we finish with this concept, we have one other important question: What is the meaning, or purpose, of life for you? Your answer, of course, probably relates to the main values or goals you have identified.

If you imagine yourself on your deathbed sometime in the distant future, what are you going to want to look back on in your life and say, "Yes, I am so glad I did that/ experienced that/had that/saw that"?

If fear shows up around this topic, just take a few deep breaths and remember that this is a lifelong journey to think about and figure out. Stay curious about it! The beauty of this question is that it can change throughout your life—and there's not really a right or wrong answer to it. Your meaning of life right now might be to experience new things and to constantly challenge yourself. It might be to see the world. It might be to help others and make the world a better place. It might be to innovate and create and leave a mark on the world through technology, art, writing, sports, or otherwise. Your meaning could be in having a family one day and passing on what you know to others in your life.

Use the space below to jot down a few ideas for what the meaning or purpose of life is, right now, for you, and let this help you through some of your most challenging or stressful moments.

_____

_____

_____

_____

_____

_____

_____

life is messy...and messy can be funny 16

let's get started

There's real value in not being perfect. It makes you human, and helps people to connect with you.

There can also be real value in using a little bit of humor to acknowledge that you aren't perfect and that your life isn't perfect. Mistakes and imperfections don't define us, and acknowledging them with a bit of humor and self-deprecation shows confidence in the fact that you know that being an imperfect human is okay, and that sometimes life is funny, even at its toughest moments.

Even though we try our hardest, the truth is that sometimes we will all still come up short. We wouldn't be human if this weren't true. So the next time you find yourself coming up short, try laughing at yourself and notice how this can help ease tensions in the people around, you and help you to connect with them—because usually, in some way or another, they've been there too. Admitting our own imperfections can be one of the most liberating moments in life.

Learning to laugh at yourself and your situation can help you to stop worrying and getting stuck in the difficult parts of life. When you accept that things can and *will* go wrong, you become free to shift your focus to a more positive and lighthearted worldview.

let's try it

Imagine during tough times that you are a character in a sitcom. Think of some of your favorite shows and how often the main characters make mistakes or have something unpleasant happen to them. But it's all part of the story! You might not yet know how your own story ends, but why not make it a bit funny along the way? Here are a few questions to ask yourself as you try writing your script:

1. Consider the alternative choices to laughter (anger, withdrawing, etc.). Will those reactions change anything about the situation?

2. In the past, has overthinking about your mistakes helped to fix or change your situation at all, or did this end up causing you more stress or frustration?

3. Think of a time you made a mistake that you have now made a certain peace with, but that you struggled with a lot when it originally happened. In this situation, eventually you came to a point where you accepted the mistake and learned to forgive yourself. In the time between the mistake happening and the moment of acceptance, did beating yourself up and dragging out the process of acceptance and forgiveness fix anything, or did it make it more painful? As you realize this, try giving yourself permission to speed up the process and be more compassionate with yourself.

Now pick out a moment in your life, either one that's already happened or one that you are worried is going to happen someday, and write it down like a script from a sitcom, throwing in a few jokes and humor as you go! It doesn't have to be completely brilliant, just a bit lighthearted. Here's a quick example from Ryan's experience:

(Ryan completely messes up the answer to a question in class.)

Friends: (*laughing*) Way to go, Ryan!

Ryan: (*laughs as well*) Yeah, I must have missed the memo on that one. Next time I'm going to make sure I don't miss my morning coffee.

Friends: Yah, quit sleeping through class! Although it's great entertainment for the rest of us.

Ryan: Don't worry, I'm here to entertain! You know class wouldn't be as much fun without me! (*All laugh together.*)

Try your own below!

Situation (past or future concern): _____

_____

What fun or humorous spin can you put on the situation to help yourself connect with the imperfect nature of being human?

_____

_____

_____

_____

_____

_____

_____

_____

more to try

One of my favorite exercises to unstick the brain when it gets stuck in the negatives is to play a little game. You can use a little humor with it, too. Be as outrageous as you like, make up a little story, or simply stretch your brain in a way that may help you see that, even when things are bad, there are still things to be grateful for.

This exercise is called "It Could Be Worse." Whenever things aren't going the way you hoped, or you find your brain focusing on mistakes you've made, play this little game of "It Could Be Worse."

Let's try a few!

Example: You got a failing grade on the quiz that was given out last week for science class.

Try: It could be worse…you could have failed the whole class. Right now, you can still bring your grade up!

Example: You found out the person you like has a crush on someone else.

Try: It could be worse…there are still a few other people you have your eye on, and lots of time to keep searching for someone who likes you back!

Try your own below.

What's a time that you can think of that wasn't the greatest?

_____

_____

What "It Could Be Worse" spin can you put on that instance?

_____

_____

_____

This activity is great when it is paired up with a gratitude journal. While unsticking from the negative side of difficult things in your life or tough times, it can also be a good mental exercise to actively focus on the good things in your life. Try writing down at least three things every day that you are grateful for. Write down a few things that you are grateful for right now to try it out:

_____

_____

_____

_____

_____

_____

_____

Goal 5

Staying Focused

17 SMART goals

let's get started

The best way to stay on track even in the face of difficult obstacles is to have SMART goals. SMART goals help us make sure that we have a really clear road map and that we know where we're going. What does SMART stand for, you ask?

S—Specific. If you only have a vague sense of what your goal is, it will make it very hard to achieve it. Something like "I want to be a better person" is so vague, it's hard to know what that looks like. Maybe what you really mean is that you want to be a more helpful person, for instance. So then think about what specific idea fits with a goal of becoming more helpful. Maybe to reach this goal, you decide you want to start volunteering.

M—Measurable. While knowing you want to start volunteering is a good start, how do you know if you are meeting a goal? Is volunteering once good enough? Or once a week? Make it measurable—a way that you can clearly tell if you are meeting your own expectations or not. Maybe you want to volunteer for three hours a week. That way you can definitely tell if you are on track for that goal.

A—Attainable. Make sure you stay realistic about your goals. If you set a goal of wanting to volunteer for ten hours a week knowing that you also have school, homework, chores, friends, and a part-time job—you probably are going to fall short of that goal or burn yourself out. Give yourself something reasonable to try to achieve.

R—Relevant. Make sure your goal is in alignment with your values and your overall big picture in life. For example, if you volunteer at a charity BBQ with your friends and only chat with them, you may be falling short of your big-picture goal of being more confident. While this may still be a fine thing to do, if you wanted to work on your confidence, it might make more sense to volunteer somewhere without your friends, so that you meet new people and get new experiences helping others.

T—Timely. Give yourself a guideline on when you want to achieve this goal. The timeline should be realistic—not so tight that you can't achieve it, but not so far away that you never end up taking action. For volunteering, you might want to give yourself a month to research and contact six different options. Giving yourself one day to figure it all out would probably be too short, but three months seems much too long. If you research and visit two options a week, by the end of the month you can probably get started.

let's try it

Now, try your own SMART goal for something important in your life!

What is a goal that you have?

_____

S—How can you make this goal specific—not vague, but clear and precise?

_____

M—How can you make sure that you can measure your progress toward this goal? What measurement tool can you use and how will you keep track of your progress?

_____

A—Double check that your goal is within your reach. You can get discouraged if you set the bar too high and miss the goal you had set for yourself. Always start with smaller steps for your goal. If those steps are really easy to reach, then you can move forward to the next step ahead of schedule.

_____

R—Step back and think of the bigger picture. Does this goal fit with a healthy, balanced, big picture of what you want for your life, and why? Are there any risks to attaining this goal—or not attaining it?

_____

_____

T—What is your timeline for achieving this goal? Do you need to break it down into steps to get started? What timeline will you set for each smaller step? How will you keep track of your timeline progress?

_____

_____

more to try

Once you have a goal, you will likely find roadblocks in your way. One of the best exercises to get started on a goal despite difficulties or setbacks is to employ a variation of the "What If" to "I Can" exercise we learned earlier in the book. Let's look at an example.

SMART goal: Wanting to gain acceptance to a high-level baseball team by next year.

What could go wrong? Getting an injury, running into politics on the team, struggling with some of the drills or with performance, or dealing with anxiety at big games.

What might you do in response to each of these problems if they do happen?

Injury—Make sure to take top care of the injury and do physiotherapy as instructed to gain back full strength and mobility. Don't push it and make it worse—extend your goal timeline if the injury requires an adjustment.

Politics—Talk to a mentor or parent about what to do to handle unpleasant or complicated politics. Write down your thoughts and try to leave intense situations if they are escalating, in order to give yourself time to think about how to react. Consider switching teams if necessary.

Drills and Performance—Build in extra practice time or cross-train with another sport to help with reflexes, balance, or strength training. Consider hiring someone for a few private training sessions if possible.

Anxiety—Talk to a counselor or mentor about strategies to gain confidence and achieve peak performance. Read some articles on the subject and talk to others who have had this experience. Practice mindfulness and breathing exercises and review other strength-building exercises from this book.

Okay, now it's your turn. Think of your SMART goal from the last section that you filled out. Now, brainstorm a few ideas of what could go wrong or what roadblocks you might run into as you start to work on this SMART goal plan.

_____

_____

_____

_____

_____

_____

What are some of the strategies you could use to overcome each of these roadblocks?

Roadblock #1: _____

_____

Roadblock #2: _____

_____

If you run into trouble figuring out possible strategies to overcome a particular roadblock, remember that you can always ask a loved one or mentor for some advice on what to do.

let's get started

One of the things that can keep us stuck instead of being able to deal with whatever comes our way in life is our natural tendency to avoid discomfort. Sometimes we can fall into the trap of avoiding difficult emotions, uncertainties, and vulnerabilities instead of continuing on toward our goals.

Think of some of the things you end up doing instead of the uncomfortable thing you're avoiding (for example, watching TV or playing video games instead of studying for a test). These ways the brain gets us to avoid things can be broken down into "DOTS." Those letters stand for Distraction, Opting Out, Thinking Strategies, and Substance Use (Harris, 2009).

Distraction is when we do things to take our minds off of other things. In small doses, distraction can sometimes be helpful if we are feeling overwhelmed—but when it keeps us from our goals, it can be harmful. These are usually fairly obvious, such as TV or games, but they can also include "helpful" distractions that get out of hand, such as less-necessary chores or to-do list items that could wait until the uncomfortable priority is completed (for example, cleaning your room instead of studying the night before a test).

Opting Out is when we simply choose not to do the thing that makes us uncomfortable. If you feel nervous about going to a party, and in order to stop feeling nervous you decide not to go (even though you really wanted to go), that's opting out.

Thinking Strategies is probably the hardest one to catch, because in small doses thinking strategies can be great. In fact, this book itself teaches you several different valuable thinking strategies. These can become a problem, though, when we get stuck in a thousand different ways of thinking about something, and never get ourselves to the *action* part of the equation. When thinking strategies take over, and we sit and think and think and think for hours, we are often using this as a different way of avoiding the actual issue itself, and never end up taking action.

Substance Use includes using anything mood altering that temporarily causes us to avoid our feelings or emotions. Things like alcohol, drugs, cigarettes, and even food and sex can fall into this category. These things distract us or numb out difficult emotions temporarily, but they usually take us further away from our goals.

let's try it

Distraction:

What are some distraction techniques you have used in the past to avoid doing things—things you have done to "zone out" or "take your mind off things" in the past?

_____

_____

_____

_____

_____

Opting Out:

What are some times you have opted out on difficult or uncomfortable things—events, activities, new experiences, interests, opportunities, or people—in an effort to avoid feeling bad?

_____

_____

_____

_____

_____

Thinking Strategies:

Check off which of the following thinking strategies you have used in the past to try to think your way out of feeling a certain way, while instead you were actually avoiding feeling or doing something important—and getting lost in your head instead.

☐ Thinking about the future or the past

☐ Worrying about something

☐ Thinking of alternate, nonexistent scenarios

☐ Thinking about escape scenarios or revenge scenarios

☐ Blaming others or yourself

☐ Thinking negatively about yourself or others

☐ Thinking of "if only" scenarios

☐ Thinking about all the unfairness in the world

☐ Analyzing yourself or others

☐ Other: _____

☐ Other: _____

☐ Other: _____

Substance Use:

List the substances you may have used to avoid feeling a certain way or doing a certain thing (for example, food, drugs, alcohol, cigarettes):

_____

_____

_____

When you think about how each of these DOTS has changed your life—for good, bad, or not at all—what do you find? Did they help you or hinder you regarding the direction you want your life to go in?

☐ Helped   ☐ Hindered

Our brain often wants us to try a lot of different ways to stop feeling uncomfortable—but this doesn't mean that we have to let these ways take total control of us! With practice, and awareness of these DOTS, you can start to catch your patterns and step into change. You can connect with what is important to you and follow your path in life, staying aligned with your goals despite obstacles.

The strategies that help you to withstand the DOTS and stay connected to your goals are many of the ones we have used so far in this book—emotion regulation, mindfulness, distress tolerance, inner narratives and dialogues, and using the resources around you to help, such as self-care and supportive relationships. But the first step to regaining control over your DOTS is to notice when they are happening!

more to try

Try answering the questions below to help you connect to this ability to move toward what is important to you, *even while having* difficult thoughts, body sensations, or emotions. This can help you find the strength to withstand the temptation to fall into one of the DOTS in the heat of a difficult situation. Think of a specific goal to help with this exercise—perhaps getting a certain grade in a class or applying for an after-school job.

1. What is important to you—what are your values connected to your goals? Why are your goals important to you?

   _____

   _____

   _____

2. What *internal* things get in the way of moving toward your values in your life? What fears, thoughts, or internal sensations often keep you from pursuing or working toward things that connect you to your values in life?

   _____

   _____

   _____

3. What are some of the DOTS that keep you from moving toward your goals in your *external* life?

   _____

   _____

   _____

4. Lastly, what are some of the things you can do or have been able to do to move toward your values and goals in life, *even during the times* that the uncomfortable internal stuff shows up?

    _____

    _____

    _____

It is this last response that is so important: things you can do *even during the times that discomfort shows up*. We always will have discomfort as part of our lives—the trick is to lean into that discomfort and find ways, such as these kinds of exercises we have worked through together, to create change and to live the life *you* want to live.

19 keeping the inner critic in check

let's get started

One of the things we haven't talked about much yet is our *Inner Critic*. When we set ourselves up for success and then something difficult comes up, our Inner Critic is the little part of us that chimes in and tells us, "I told you so. There was no way you were ever going to be able to do this. You thought you could handle this? No way are you talented enough, tough enough, or good enough. Just give up now."

When life throws you curveballs, the last thing you need is to let that Inner Critic take over and steer you away from pursuing your goals.

The first step here is recognizing that this voice is only one small part among all the parts in our head. Have you seen the movie *Inside Out*? (If you haven't, watch it right away!) Our brains really are like that movie—we have different "parts" and personalities that sometimes take the wheel in our head. But the good news is, once we learn the different characters in our minds, we can start to change the conversation.

It's important to identify our Inner Critic, so we are aware when it might be taking over. Now, even though it can be pretty nasty or disheartening when it shows up, the good news is that your Inner Critic is *technically* trying to help you. It just has a funny way of going about it sometimes. The Inner Critic is often trying to keep you from getting hurt—from becoming vulnerable or taking chances or looking foolish—so it tries to be super tough on you to keep you safe. When your system is overwhelmed or doesn't know what to do, the Inner Critic may show up and try to help. The problem is that, without boundaries and rules, it can run away with the system and get out of hand. It can become hurtful or harmful, and can inadvertently hurt you more on the inside than any experience in the real world might have hurt you in reality. Hopefully, once you can see this, it can help you change the relationship with that voice in your head.

This is why we need to learn to keep it in check—to make sure it sticks to doing its *actual* job and doesn't give itself a promotion. Its actual job is just to keep you alert and watching out for threats to yourself and your system—not to beat you down and paralyze you and take away all your confidence. That's a little too much power in the hands of the Inner Critic—so let's explore how to keep that little voice in check.

let's try it

To start with, I want you to think of what that Inner Critic in your own head might look like. Personally, I imagine a little green gremlin guy with stumpy little legs and a devil's tail. Yours could look like anything—a creature, a person, a cartoon, or something else entirely. Draw it out below. (You don't have to be an amazing artist, just draw something that represents the idea you have in your head!)

Now, what does its voice sound like? You may have thought it sounded like, well, *you*, but now think a little bit more. This little character probably has its own voice, too. My gremlin has a funny, scratchy, high-pitched voice. It's actually pretty funny, and that takes some of the punch out of what that Inner Critic sometimes says, and helps me keep things in perspective. Write what yours sounds like here.

Now, what does your Inner Critic often say, especially in tough times or when you run into obstacles in life? Things like "Don't bother, it's not going to work out," or maybe things like "Nobody cares about you anyway." Knowing the catch phrases of your particular Inner Critic is crucial to being able to know when it has taken over the driver's seat in your mind. Write down a few lines you might recognize as coming from your Inner Critic.

_____

_____

Now let's see if we can make that Inner Critic seem less scary, less intimidating. After all, we did make this character up in our own heads. So as we learned earlier in this book, we can change the story!

Try drawing a little Inner Critic that looks similar to the first one, but also a bit silly or funny. Remember, you're actually the one in control of this story here.

```




```

Now what would that new creature's voice sound like?

_____

The next time your Inner Critic pops up, I want you to remember this picture.

But how can you tell if it's your Inner Critic that pops up in your head, as opposed to your true inner voice? That can be really hard sometimes.

To figure this out, it can help to compare how we are talking in our own heads to ourselves versus how we would support or talk to a friend instead.

What do you say to a friend if they are struggling, or feeling upset, hurt, or lonely?

_____

_____

_____

What do you say to *yourself* if you are struggling, upset, hurt, or lonely?

_____

_____

_____

If these are different, this is your clue that your Inner Critic is showing up instead of your true voice.

Sometimes we get tricked into a false belief that the only way to get ourselves to do something is to be hard on ourselves or we are going to fail. We think that we need to yell at ourselves to get results. But when you think about it, you wouldn't do that to your friends, because it would hurt their feelings. It would hurt your relationship with them, and they wouldn't trust you or feel as close to you in the future. The same thing applies when you're talking to yourself.

Try rewriting the things that you would say to a friend who was upset or struggling, but this time write those things to yourself.

_____

_____

_____

_____

Try actually saying one of these things out loud to yourself in a mirror. I know, it might sound weird, but trust me when I say that at some point it should feel totally natural to say something positive, encouraging, and kind to yourself in a mirror. Remember that arm-crossing exercise at the beginning of this book. This might feel weird at first, but it's an important step toward change.

Use this exercise to help keep that Inner Critic in check when you find yourself struggling with difficult times. Let that Inner Critic know that you are actually the one in charge, that you are running the ship inside your brain. Briefly listen, acknowledge, and then politely decline the Inner Critic's advice, thanking it for trying to protect you, but letting it know that you've actually got things under control, even if things aren't perfect, or even if things get tough or messy. You have the tools and the ability to get through it!

more to try

When life gets difficult and things aren't going our way, or when we screw up, or when people are mad at us, it can be hard to remember the positive things about ourselves. When someone has a strong negative opinion about us, it can be a challenge to remember that opinions aren't always facts, and that everyone has both strengths and weaknesses—and that, despite our imperfections, we are always, always worthy and worthwhile. Once we curb our Inner Critic, we also want to access and remember our strengths.

So let's get a clearer picture of all the awesome things that make you *you*, so that you can remember that this isn't up for debate, even in the most challenging times in your life.

I want you to think of all the positive things about yourself that you can possibly think of—traits, qualities, values, accomplishments, strengths, physical attributes, skills, talents—anything and everything that could be considered a positive—and write them down on the next page. I also want you to think of positive things that your friends, family members, or other people in your life might say about you if we were to ask them, and add those into this list as well. If you're not sure what they would say, go out and actually ask them! If you get stuck, don't worry; it doesn't mean there *isn't* anything to add to the list. Your brain is probably just out of practice and needs a bit more time or some external support to break down some mental blocks to doing this exercise. You can also flip back through the other exercises in this book and find some likely answers there, too.

_____

_____

_____

_____

_____

_____

_____

_____

_____

_____

_____

_____

_____

_____

_____

_____

_____

_____

_____

_____

_____

Most of us don't spend nearly enough time thinking of the positives about ourselves, and we really do need to practice it. The homework I recommend is that you keep coming back to this positive list about yourself and continue to add to it, review it, and think about it, at least three times a day. For example, once at every meal time, or once in the morning when you wake up, once at night before bed, and at least one other time during the day. This is a really good brain-stretching exercise!

As this list grows, copy it out and keep it with you, take a picture and put it on your phone, or download my app PositiveU, and keep your list in there. You can find it on your app store on your phone or tablet.

end of book check-in 20

Let's check in again on that very first thing we did together—the little check-in chart of resilience measures near the beginning of this book. We have worked through a whole ton of ideas and concepts that should've helped you improve in each area!

Have a look again at each of the items, and circle the number on the right that you feel *best* fits how you feel about each item *now* (from 0 = completely false to 4 = completely true).

Statement	Rating
I generally feel strong and capable of overcoming challenges.	0...1...2....3...4
When I get stressed, I usually bounce back fairly quickly.	0...1...2....3...4
I generally stay calm and steady when the going gets tough.	0...1...2....3...4
I am generally flexible, meaning if my usual way of doing things isn't working, I am ready and willing to try something else.	0...1...2....3...4
I am able to see that even the most difficult situations will pass, using humor or optimism to see the "big picture" of my life.	0...1...2....3...4
I like myself for who I am inside and think well of myself.	0...1...2....3...4
Difficult times don't change the way I feel about myself for the worse.	0...1...2....3...4
I know when to seek help or support, and where to find it.	0...1...2....3...4
I am good at reaching out and connecting with people when I need support.	0...1...2....3...4
I usually try to solve my problems, but I know how to accept and cope if something is beyond my control, even when it's hard.	0...1...2....3...4
I anticipate difficult situations, make a plan, and stay focused and carry out my plan even when stressed.	0...1...2....3...4

Statement	Rating
I am good at coping with strong negative emotions.	0...1...2....3...4
I have goals and am optimistic about my future, even if I run into obstacles.	0...1...2....3...4
I believe I've grown stronger from what I've experienced, and that stress can make me a stronger person.	0...1...2....3...4
I don't beat myself up when my best efforts don't succeed.	0...1...2....3...4
I stay focused and think clearly under pressure. I am persistent, determined, and resolved.	0...1...2....3...4
Total Score (add the scores from the right-hand column):	

How did it go? When you look back at your first chart, did some of these items shift over to the right side of the scale? Did your total tally at the bottom increase? I hope so, because you've done a lot of work here, and you deserve to feel more in control, more confident, more flexible and adaptable, and more able to get through anything life might throw your way.

If you notice some areas where you still need to improve, you might want to revisit the activities in this workbook. Practice makes perfect!

Through this workbook, you now have a whole set of tools to better understand yourself, your life, and the meaning and values behind everything that you do. Some of the things you have learned are:

1. To understand yourself and your "story"—and know your ability to rewrite this story

2. To understand the different "parts" of yourself that show up in different circumstances and different moods, and how to shift in and out of those different "parts" of yourself

3. To understand the internal voice that shows up in different moods, and how to change this conversation through externalizing and talking back to an unhelpful inner voice

4. To be aware of your most classic go-to DOTS that you fall prey to when you start to get uncomfortable

5. To know your values and what drives you, your purpose, and the meaning of your life

6. To connect with your values, to lean into the discomfort, and to change and challenge your story and your "sticky brain," in order to live the life that *you* want to live

You have the resilience to make it through anything. You have the power to change your life, your story, and your meaning—always. When you rewrite your story, sometimes it can be hard to say goodbye to old parts of yourself. So give yourself time to be sad, to grieve, and even to mourn for the things that you have to let go of. But be willing to let go of things that are no longer helpful to you. Be willing to step into the next part of your life and to get uncomfortable, to challenge your brain to let go, and to lean into the discomfort of life. Where discomfort lives is where strength and growth blossom. You have so much to give this world. Let yourself write your story in a way that allows you to unlock the real, true "inner you."

You got this!

Signing off,

Cheryl M. Bradshaw

acknowledgements

First and foremost, I want to thank you, dear reader, for working through this book with me. Working through this kind of stuff that we talk about in this book can be hard, and your dedication, persistence, and *resilience* in working through each of these exercises is the whole reason I do what I do, and create the books I create! Thanks for being awesome!

Thank you especially to New Harbinger, my publisher, for the opportunity to reach a larger audience in a broader scope than I might have ever been able to do on my own. My whole goal in life is to try to help people – however I can – and this platform has been truly a blessing to try to continue to meet that goal. New Harbinger's dedication to helping people through their broad array of published works focusing on mental health and wellbeing is inspiring, and I count myself lucky to be amongst their distinguished authors.

Thank you to Elizabeth Hollis Hansen, my acquisitions editor, in helping to make this book and this vision a reality, as well as to Ken Knabb for the editing work and many emails back and forth to make this book what it is today. I also want to thank my agent, Arnold Gosewich, for taking that first leap of faith with me as a new author on my first book, *How to Like Yourself,* and for your ongoing work with me through many phone calls and emails and brainstorming sessions for this book and future projects.

I want to send a huge shout-out and giant thank you to Ryan Miller, who created the images you see in this book. He has always been a huge supporter of my work, and has lent his computer skills to help me out in the areas I have far less (if any!) expertise. He has helped me out through many technology-based questions I have sent his way, and he is always up for a conversation about my work and the latest projects. Thanks, Ryan!

A big thank you to my parents, Mary Ann and Michael, for being my ongoing listening ears, unofficial editors, and ever-ready sounding boards for this and many other projects I have taken on. Many ideas were run past you both to create the final outcome readers are able to enjoy today. Your help throughout my life has been immeasurable. Thank you both for always being there and supporting me.

Lastly, a big thank you to my husband, Andrew, and my two doggos, Darwin and Kiara, for always being there for hugs, snuggles, and emotional support on the days where things felt overwhelming or heavy, and for celebrations when things were going well. I think it's time for one more big celebration now!

Aloba, O., O. Olabisi, and T. Aloba. 2016. "The 10-Item Connor-Davidson Resilience Scale: Factorial Structure, Reliability, Validity, and Correlates Among Student Nurses in Southwestern Nigeria." *Journal of the American Psychiatric Nurses Association 22*: 43–51.

Campbell-Sills, L., and M. B. Stein. 2007. "Psychometric Analysis and Refinement of the Connor-Davidson Resilience Scale (CD-RISC): Validation of a 10-Item Measure of Resilience." *Journal of Traumatic Stress 20*: 1019–1028.

Cicchetti, D., and F. A. Rogosch. 2009. "Adaptive Coping Under Conditions of Extreme Stress: Multilevel Influences on the Determinants of Resilience in Maltreated Children." *New Directions for Child and Adolescent Development 2009*: 47–59.

Connor, K. M., and J. R. Davidson. 2003. "Development of a New Resilience Scale: The Connor-Davidson Resilience Scale (CD-RISC)." *Depression and Anxiety 18*: 76–82.

Doré, B. P., J. Weber, and K. N. Ochsner. 2017. "Neural Predictors of Decisions to Cognitively Control Emotion." *Journal of Neuroscience 37*: 2580–2588.

Duckworth, A. L., C. Peterson, M. D. Matthews, and D. R. Kelly. 2007. "Grit: Perseverance and Passion for Long-Term Goals." *Journal of Personality and Social Psychology 92*: 1087–1101.

Eisenberger, N. I., M. Lieberman, and K. D. Williams. 2003. "Does Rejection Hurt? An fMRI Study of Social Exclusion." *Science (New York, NY) 302*: 290–292. 10.1126 /science.1089134

Greenberger, D., and C. Padesky. 2015. *Mind Over Mood: Change How You Feel By Changing The Way You Think* (2nd Ed). New York: The Guilford Press.

Harris, R. 2009. *ACT Made Simple: An Easy-To-Read Primer on Acceptance and Commitment Therapy.* Oakland, California: New Harbinger Publications.

Kalisch, R., M. B. Müller, and O. Tüscher. 2015. "A Conceptual Framework for the Neurobiological Study of Resilience." *Behavioral Brain Science 38*: e92. 10.1017 /S0140525X1400082X

Margolis, H., and P. McCabe. 2006. "Improving Self-Efficacy and Motivation: What to Do, What to Say." *Intervention in School and Clinic 41*: 218–227.

McGonigal, K. 2013. "How to Make Stress Your Friend." https://www.ted.com/talks/kelly_mcgonigal_how_to_make_stress_your_friend

McKay, M. 2007. *DBT Skills Workbook*. Oakland, California: New Harbinger Publications.

Padesky, C. 1997. "A More Effective Treatment Focus for Social Phobia?" *International Cognitive Therapy Newsletter* 11(1): 1-3.

Peres, J., A. Moreira-Almeida, A. Nasello, and H. Koenig. 2007. "Spirituality and Resilience in Trauma Victims." *Journal of Religion and Health* 46: 343–350.

Schwartz, R. C. 1997. *Internal Family Systems Therapy*. New York: The Guilford Press.

Schiraldi, G. R. (2017). *The Resilience Workbook: Essential Skills to Recover from Stress, Trauma, and Adversity*. Oakland, CA: New Harbinger Publications, Inc.

Shapiro, F. (2013). *Getting Past Your Past: Take Control of Your Life with Self-Help Techniques from EMDR Therapy*. Emmaus, Pennsylvania: Rodale Books.

Siqueira, L., and A. Diaz. 2004. "Fostering Resilience in Adolescent Females." *Mount Sinai Journal of Medicine 71*: 148–154.

Traub, F., and R. Boynton-Jarrett. 2017. "Modifiable Resilience Factors to Childhood Adversity for Clinical Pediatric Practice." *Pediatrics* 139: e20162569, 10.1542/peds.2016–2569.

Windle, G., G. Bennett, and K. M. Noyes. 2011. "A Methodological Review of Resilience Measurement Scales." *Health and Quality of Life Outcomes 9*: 1–18.

Wolin, S. J., and S. Wolin. 1993. *The Resilient Self: How Survivors of Troubled Families Arise Above Adversity*. New York: Villard.

Yeager, D. S., and C. S. Dweck. 2012. "Mindsets that Promote Resilience: When Students Believe that Personal Characteristics Can Be Developed." *Educational Psychologist 47*: 302–314.

Cheryl M. Bradshaw, MA, is a registered psychotherapist working in private practice, and author of *How to Like Yourself*—a self-esteem guide for teens that was a #1 new release in its category on Amazon. She has been featured on various television shows, radio shows, and podcasts, including *Breakfast Television*, Global's *The Morning Show*, CBC Radio, and *Today's Parent*. Her book was also selected as a 2016 Foreword INDIES Finalist for the 2016 Young Adult Nonfiction category. In addition, Cheryl received the inaugural Outstanding Alumni Award from Yorkville University in 2017. Cheryl served as a counselor at both Sheridan College and the University of Guelph. She also has a background in teaching, and continues to work with and volunteer with schools and charities to talk about youth and young adult mental health, self-esteem, and also to support parents with their teens.

Cheryl resides in Hamilton, ON, Canada, with her husband Andrew and their dogs, Darwin and Kiara. Find out more about Cheryl at www.cherylmbradshaw.com, and on social media @cherylmbradshaw.

To keep working on some of the concepts you have learned throughout, download the app, PositiveU, a great complement to *How to Like Yourself* and the *Resilience Workbook for Teens*.

More ⏱ Instant Help Books for Teens

An Imprint of New Harbinger Publications

**DON'T LET YOUR EMOTIONS
RUN YOUR LIFE FOR TEENS**

Dialectical Behavior Therapy Skills
for Helping You Manage Mood
Swings, Control Angry Outbursts &
Get Along with Others

978-1572248830 / US $17.95

**THE ANXIETY
WORKBOOK FOR TEENS**

Activities to Help You Deal with
Anxiety & Worry

978-1572246034 / US $15.95

**MINDFULNESS FOR
TEEN DEPRESSION**

A Workbook for
Improving Your Mood

978-1626253827 / US $16.95

STUFF THAT SUCKS

A Teen's Guide to Accepting What
You Can't Change & Committing to
What You Can

978-1626258655 / US $12.95

PUT WORRIES HERE

A Creative Journal for Teens
with Anxiety

978-1684032143 / US $16.95

**THE GRIT GUIDE
FOR TEENS**

A Workbook to Help You Build
Perseverance, Self-Control &
a Growth Mindset

978-1626258563 / US $16.95

🌱 **newharbinger**publications
1-800-748-6273 / newharbinger.com

(VISA, MC, AMEX / prices subject to change without notice)

Follow Us [f] [𝕏] [📷] [P]

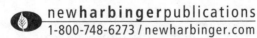

Don't miss out on new books in the subjects that interest you.
Sign up for our **Book Alerts** at **newharbinger.com/bookalerts**